OPPORTU

in

Acting
Careers

REVISED EDITION

DICK MOORE

McGraw·Hill

*New York   Chicago   San Francisco   Lisbon   London   Madrid   Mexico City
Milan   New Delhi   San Juan   Seoul   Singapore   Sydney   Toronto*

Library of Congress Cataloging-in-Publication Data

Moore, Dick.
     Opportunities in acting careers / Dick Moore.— Rev. ed.
        p.   cm.
     ISBN 0-07-143845-9
     1. Acting—Vocational guidance—United States.   I. Title.

   PN2055.M6   2005
   792.02'8'02373—dc22   2004025941

2 3 4 5 6 7 8 9 0   DOC/DOC   0 9 8 7 6 5

ISBN 0-07-143845-9

Interior design by Rattray Design

McGraw-Hill books are available at special quantity discounts to use as premiums and sales promotions, or for use in corporate training programs. For more information, please write to the Director of Special Sales, Professional Publishing, McGraw-Hill, Two Penn Plaza, New York, NY 10121-2298. Or contact your local bookstore.

This book is printed on acid-free paper.

Contents

FOREWORD

THAT AEOLIAN HARP of actors, Montgomery Clift, once said to me, "Acting is a great art and a crappy profession." And one day that most durable of actresses, Ruth Gordon, advised, "It is not just enough to have talent—ya gotta know what to do with it!"

My dear friend of many years, Dick Moore, has provided a valuable guide to this "art" and "profession" called acting. It is a remarkable achievement, for in the most succinct, compassionate, and knowledgeable manner it gives the aspiring performer extremely useful advice.

I have long thought that schools, classes, and many teachers almost completely ignore the nuts and bolts of the job: how to make a living and how to navigate the labyrinth of the profession's ups and downs.

This volume of Dick Moore's is a careful, accurate, and realistic guide to the profession of acting. It is a handbook that will be of great value to those who have been possessed by that irresistible urge to act—that indefinable urge that has driven many talented young people to the pinnacle of fame and fortune and others less gifted to lives of sacrifice and disappointment.

Because of its very nature, the profession of acting has always been surrounded by an aura of glamour, a hypnotizing, magnetic attraction that has drawn certain people to it with an overpowering force, causing them to make great personal sacrifices to bathe in its flattering light and to bow to its thrilling applause.

But, unfortunately, too many of the people who are so captivated by acting are unaware of its down-to-earth side—its business side—that must necessarily be a part of every actor's daily life.

If you wish to pursue a career in the acting profession . . . if you want a realistic insight into all phases of the business of acting, this guide will give you the facts you need and answer your questions. After reading this book, you will realize that acting can be one of the most wonderful professions, and it can also be one of the most precarious of pursuits. There will be periods of searching, unsuccessful auditions and interviews, of losing a part to someone else, and periods of intense discouragement. But there will also be moments of elation, of personal fulfillment, of rising to undreamed of heights of fame and economic success.

If the urge to act is strong enough within you and if you are blessed with the necessary talent, you will be sustained through the ups and downs that are the lot of all actors . . . and you may reach the coveted goal of success.

You will realize, too, that to be an actor you also have to be a human being. You will have to seek education and culture, and you will have to develop a deep understanding and affection for human nature.

I remember my beginnings very well. I also remember each heartache and obstacle. But someday, you may say, as I do, that it's worth it.

—Roddy McDowall

Acknowledgments

The author gratefully acknowledges the generous assistance of the following in the preparation of this book:

Actors' Equity Association, American Federation of Television and Radio Artists (AFTRA), Arena Stage, Conrad Bain, Theodore Bikel, CBS Radio Network, Ossie Davis, Philip Hayes Dean, Amy Dolan, Conard Fowkes, Nancy Fox, Micki Grant, Richard Grayson, Kim Roberts Hedgpeth, Anne Jackson, Michel Kinter, Jerome Lawrence, the League of American Theatres and Producers, Lincoln Center Repertory Company, Terry Marone, Gareth May, John McGuire, NBC Television Network, Diane Nichols, Guy Pace, Jean-Paul Richard, Andy Schefman, Screen Actors Guild, Martin E. Segal Company, John Sucke, Terry Walker.

With special thanks to my friend and associate, Helaine Feldman.

1

THERE'S NO BUSINESS
LIKE SHOW BUSINESS

SWIMMING POOLS; PRIVATE jets; multimillion dollar contracts; homes in California, New York, the Caribbean. The cast of "Friends" earned $1 million per episode; Tom Cruise gets $20 million per film. Sounds wonderful—and easy. It is wonderful. But it's not easy.

For every performer who earns millions of dollars, there are thousands who earn below the poverty level. In Actors' Equity Association (the union of stage actors) for example, the median annual earnings for its more than forty-five thousand members is about $6,000 per year.

Screen Actors Guild (SAG) has similar figures for its ninety thousand members. While seven-digit movie deals make headlines for some stars—creating a false impression that all actors are highly paid—the reality is far less glamorous.

The other downsides are the almost constant travel, lack of traditional or "normal" family life, loss of privacy, obsession with appearance and age, and, no matter how successful, total insecurity and fear of not getting that next job.

So much for limousines and tennis courts. So much for easy.

Playwright Neil Simon (*The Odd Couple*, *Plaza Suite*, *The Sunshine Boys*) told an audience of actors:

> It's hard to be an actor. I know of no greater act of courage than to walk out on an empty stage, seeing the silhouette of four ominous figures sitting in the darkened theater, with your mouth drying and your fingers trembling, trying to keep the pages in your hand from rattling and trying to focus your eyes on the lines so you don't automatically skip the two most important speeches in the scene, and all the while trying to give a performance worthy of an opening night with only four pages of a play, the rest of which you know nothing about. And then to finally get through it, only to hear from the voice in the darkened theater, "Thank you . . ." It has got to be the most painful, frustrating, and fearful experience in the world. Because with it comes a 90 percent chance of rejection. And to do it time after time, year after year, even after you've proven yourself in show after show, requires more than courage and fearlessness. It requires such dedication to your craft and to the work you've chosen for your life, that I'm sure if Equity posted a sign backstage that said, "Any actor auditioning for this show who gets turned down will automatically be shot," you'd still only get about a 12 percent turnaway.

What is this career that you've chosen all about?

Announce to your family and friends that you want to be an actor, and more likely than not you will be met with anything from downright horror to an indulgent chuckle intended to indicate that, although you may be master of your fate, you are, nonetheless, not completely in command of all your faculties. It's the rare family that accepts the news that one of its members intends to become an actor with the same tranquility that is reserved for an announcement of intentions to become a doctor, a lawyer, or an accountant.

This typical response is a residual symptom of the ancient concept of the actor as a wandering minstrel, a "thing of shreds and patches," who lived by wits and was allergic to "honest" work. This prejudice has been ingrained for a long time now, stemming from the days when there was no organized theater as such—when entertainers roamed the roads, sharing lodgings and reputations with thieves and other unsavory individuals. Today, we still witness the look or cry of disbelief following the pronouncement that someone wants to be an actor—a response that comes from the almost universal realization that unemployment is the norm, and success difficult to attain.

Then, too, you have to think carefully. Do you really want to be an "actor"? Or do you want to be a "star"? The two are not necessarily the same thing. Do you want to work live on stage, in feature films, or star in a television sitcom? There are important differences here, too. More and more, today's actors work in all media. For example, Sarah Jessica Parker was a respected stage actor long before her television show, "Sex and the City," made her a household name. Now, of course, she's in great demand as a commercial spokesperson, for film, and for other television projects. There is more money to be made in films and television, but many actors consider working before a live audience on a stage the more interesting and challenging work. Even Nicole Kidman has taken a turn on Broadway.

Historical Background

With the ascendancy of the Puritan influence, many church people were convinced that the theatrical profession encouraged immorality. Maybe they were right. Suppression of theaters was a common thing, and often the actor was forced to turn to other pursuits—not all of them socially acceptable—to earn a living.

Since America's founding fathers of the 1600s were of Puritan stock, early theater in this country had two strikes against it at the outset. In the early days of the colonial settlers, acting was actually illegal in nearly every city. One man was permitted to spend all his money building a theater in New York and then was forbidden to act in it. Gradually, some of the taboos broke down, and as the people reached out for their cultural stimulation, play-going became more common practice. By the end of the eighteenth century, there were functioning theaters in American cities and, although they had been closed during the Revolutionary War, the British, whenever they captured one, would reopen it with their own troupes. President Washington, a theatergoer himself, helped to popularize theater when the war ended, but not until the middle of the nineteenth century was it considered even remotely "acceptable" to choose acting as a profession.

Even then, actors remained suspect. Unhappily, many of the early idols of the stage themselves provided much of the ammunition for the volleys hurled against them. This was inevitable, for anyone attracted to a profession that was subjected to such social stigma had to be a nonconformist. Then, too, some of the actors may have figured that if they were going to suffer bad reputations anyway, they might as well enjoy themselves while they were at it.

The infamous John Wilkes Booth, an actor and brother of Edwin Booth, who was one of the greatest American actors, further blackened the actors' image when he assassinated President Abraham Lincoln. The historic Players Club in New York City has a copy of a letter from Edwin Booth addressed to the people of the

United States, expressing deep sorrow for the consequences of his brother's act.

The late nineteenth and early twentieth centuries saw change. Stars such as Sarah Bernhardt, Sir Henry Irving, Ellen Terry, John Drew, Maude Adams, Richard Mansfield, Lillian Russell, and Edwin Booth had achieved such recognition that acting had come to be considered one of the best rewarded and most glamorous of professions.

Producer Florenz Ziegfeld added new luster with the introduction of a new type of production, the "revue," which he launched with the Follies of 1907. This was followed annually by similar productions.

Outside New York, scores of stock and repertory companies flourished throughout the country, selling tickets at prices ranging from twenty-five cents in the balcony to $1.50 for the best orchestra seats. These groups had begun to mushroom around 1885 and continued to thrive, wounded only slightly by early radio and silent, primitive motion pictures. For the most part, these touring companies lived quite compatibly beside the "flat actors" on the movie screens. The Broadway stage was thriving, and vaudeville was also doing well. Times were good—there was enough for everybody. Southern California, with its sunny climate, infrequent rainfall, and varied, picturesque scenery attracted filmmakers in increasing numbers, magnifying and multiplying massively the glittering image of the actor already established by the stage.

Between 1928 and 1930 the roof caved in—not all at once, but it sagged slowly, battered by the double weight of talking pictures and the Wall Street crash. Vaudeville all but vanished, its lighting booths displaced by film projectors. Stock companies folded, and many Broadway theaters were dark. Hollywood's talking picture became the number-one entertainment medium, gobbling up its competition, thriving on opulence and ostentation, and dispensing for a few cents the lavish, dazzling fantasy that offered escape from the grim reality of the Great Depression.

With the development of the talking picture, the era of glamour had come to full fruition. Actors and actresses became idols through the efforts of well-organized and imaginative studio publicity departments. The lengths to which studios sometimes went to maintain the public image of their stars were, by today's standards, quite incredible. There were many instances when great pressure was placed on stars to keep them from marrying, or, if they were married, to hide that fact from their fans. For a movie star to give birth to a baby was sometimes considered treason by a studio.

Happily for actors, this condition did not last. Gradually there developed a tendency to humanize the image of actors, rather than isolate them. Again, the times were changing. When the president of the United States served hot dogs on the White House lawn to the king and queen of England, Hollywood watched out of the corner of its eye. Humility was becoming chic.

Although the ivory towers of the glamour factories began to crack even prior to World War II, doubtless the war itself had the most to do with a new evolution of the actor. No longer was it fashionable to live lavishly; it was, in fact, unpatriotic. Actors donned uniforms and fought, and some were killed. Stars not in uniform entertained troops, ran stage-door canteens, grew well-publicized "victory gardens," voted in elections, and after the war, even sounded off for or against political candidates.

In short, the community of actors and their employers had come to accept that they were a part of their society, not apart from it. Society had begun to accept that acting is a profession—an art, perhaps, but not witchcraft.

Television, of course, brings the actor right into every American living room. An actor in a continuing series creates a role, becomes identified with it, and thereby becomes an instant celebrity. The actor is her or his "character," and then as a personality, the actor becomes the subject of scores of interviews on another phenomenon—the talk show. In short, where once only fan magazines churned out monthly "inside" stories about the stars, now favorite television heroes and heroines may be seen touring the networks, which eagerly reveal their most intimate "secrets."

People see a great deal of acting these days: from television and commercials to community and school plays. Broadway shows and revues have become familiar fare to almost everyone you know, especially if you live in or near a large city.

The Typical Actor

In the role today of citizen-artist, what is the average American actor like? Well, there is no "average," of course, for an actor's only commodity is her or his individuality. But we can consider a statistical average.

A recent survey of the membership of Actors' Equity Association shows that approximately 1.7 percent of the membership are under the age of 20; 58.7 percent are between the ages of 20 and 40, about 40 percent of whom are between 30 and 40; another 20 percent are between the ages of 40 and 50; and 10 percent are between 50 and 60. The remaining are over 60 years of age.

Males comprise 53 percent of the membership and females 47 percent, and about 90 percent of the membership is Caucasian.

Interestingly, too, the survey shows that about 81 percent of the union's membership of more than forty-five thousand members joined Equity in the past fifteen years.

Records show a pattern of movement from the East Coast of the United States to the central and western regions of the country over the last ten years.

Disadvantages

Let's begin with the disadvantages because, numerically at least, there appear to be more of them.

The greatest disadvantage of the acting profession is the chronic and acute shortage of jobs. Everybody knows this, but it doesn't discourage thousands of youngsters from descending on New York and Hollywood each year, eager to beat the odds. A classic story that typifies this is the one about the two unemployed actors who meet at an audition. "How are things?" one asked the other.

"Terrible," the second actor replied. "I haven't worked for six months. My unemployment compensation has run out, and the rent's not paid. My kids are sick, too. I don't know what we'll do."

"You think that's bad?" the first actor said unsympathetically. "I haven't worked since talking pictures came on the scene in 1928. You know, I'm thinking of quitting the business."

This sad, unfunny joke pretty well illustrates both actors' legendary determination to follow their chosen profession and the perils inherent in doing so. But there are other disadvantages to acting, too, some of them stemming directly from the lack of opportunity.

One of these is credit, or rather the lack of it. Not infrequently, the membership meetings of the various actors' unions have discussed ways to solve the problems of actors who have been denied bank loans, charge accounts, and credit cards because of their occupation. Often actors report that their premium rates for certain kinds of insurance were doubled and that the telephone company had demanded twice the regular deposit before installing their phones. So it appears that the prejudice we discussed earlier has not vanished, even today.

Yet banks and loan companies are notoriously unemotional, so there must be still another reason for this attitude. The basic reason for an actor's reputation as a bad credit risk lies in the completely uncertain, haphazard nature of the acting profession. Labor Department surveys show employment in the arts is very sporadic, with most performers working for many different employers during a single year. In addition, performing artists have to, and do, leave home to work at their profession; and because not enough professional work is available, most performing artists also work at other jobs outside the entertainment industry.

This is a grim picture to present to a credit officer, in whose mind it is not a question of an actor's honesty or intent. The problem is merely an awareness of the economic horrors that confront most actors at one time or another.

Eventually, performers themselves, working through and with the cooperation of their unions, took action to provide actors with a means of obtaining credit, saving, and borrowing within the framework of the unions themselves. The Actors Federal Credit Union, a federally chartered organization, was established by members of Actors' Equity in 1963 to deal effectively with the actor's perennial problems in obtaining credit, getting loans, and managing money in general. Today, the Actors Federal Credit Union serves more than fifteen thousand members, has assets of over $84 million, and is open to members of many related organizations, unions, and guilds. The credit union now includes checking accounts, access to automatic teller machines throughout the country, and a Visa credit card, as well as direct deposit, IRAs, touch-tone teller banking, CDs, and an auto-buying service. Clearly, the credit union has come a long way since it was originally chartered by a handful of actors who decided it should be easier for actors to borrow money.

Aside from the difficulty of obtaining credit, another disadvantage connected with show business is the suspicion with which outside employers frequently regard an actor, if and when he or she decides to seek other permanent employment. Some employers have been stung by an impoverished actor who decides to "give up the business." So the actor takes a "normal" job, swearing in the bargain that he or she is through with acting and can be counted on to stay in the new position. But a call for a part or even an audition comes the following week, and the "big break" cannot be ignored. Our actor quits. The fact that he or she feels apologetic about it doesn't make it easier for the next actor who applies.

Another disadvantage of the entertainment profession that must be acknowledged is the frequent instability of family life. The actor must work where and when it is possible, and frequent travel or a long stint on the road usually means that a married person is separated from her or his family. If one has children, it is difficult—and sometimes illegal—to take them out of school; even if a married couple does not have children, prolonged separations occasioned by the need for one (or both) of the partners to work in the field must certainly be considered. Very few actors are able to pick and choose their jobs based on the artistic merits of the scripts or on personal and family considerations. Usually the actor's residence is not a matter of choice, but is dictated by the need to work at each rare opportunity. Many performers have given up employment, even stardom, to devote time to children and family. Some return to "the business," and some do not. Travel often remains a constant necessity. Also, although it would seem glamorous to work in a hit television series, the hours are extremely long and the work arduous.

Some years ago, Actors' Equity conducted a workshop on stress, anxiety, and the actor. The workshop considered social and psychological difficulties that result from frequent unemployment and the problems associated with how actors' families respond to the disappointments inherent in the life of a performer. Judging from the turnout, and the fact that the workshop was necessary in the first place, the problems are both real and widespread.

Little needs to be said about the unpredictability of an actor's income. Apart from the wide variance in earnings among actors as a group, most attempts by individuals to predict their incomes a year or two in advance are purely speculative. Even reasonable expectations of employment frequently fall through, and hot deals are often cold before contracts are signed.

Today an actor may be earning many thousands of dollars a week as a regular performer on a popular television series, and living expenses may be scaled accordingly. But in just a few weeks, if the audience ratings don't promise a commercial success, the series may be canceled suddenly, leaving the cast with no income.

These are common hazards of the business, and even when the actor's average income exceeds the average salary earned in other professions, it still comes in irregular and unpredictable spurts. It's often feast or famine: during periods of unemployment, the family may go into debt; during good times, living expenses continue, back debts must be paid, and it is not always possible to lay money away for the next "dry spell." Sometimes, too, there is a tendency to deceive oneself into believing that a good job will immediately be followed by another and that secure times are just ahead; perhaps the savings left over from a good show will be used to pay for that long-wished-for vacation, automobile, or wardrobe. But when the job is over, the bills pile up again, and the cycle begins to repeat itself. The person who earns $100,000 a year certainly isn't rich;

still he or she can plan vacations, allow for some luxuries, and generally anticipate a certain standard of living. Most actors who average the same amount over a year's period can plan virtually nothing.

Nor is the tax structure merciful toward actors. Granted, certain income tax deductions are allowed, including commissions paid to agents, coaching (but only for a particular role), living expenses on the road (but only if another permanent residence is maintained elsewhere), photographs and publicity, union dues, and so on. But no consideration whatsoever is given for the costs of the long-range development of a career.

Advantages

The advantages of the profession are obvious to a successful actor and to everyone else. Nobody who reads that a film star just concluded a picture deal for $15 million, plus a share of the gross receipts, doubts that for some, acting is an immensely rewarding business. The legendary opportunities for accumulating extreme wealth, with relatively little or no capital investment to start with, have all but vanished in today's society—except for the actor and the athlete. There is always a chance that he or she will make it. Perhaps not a very good chance, to be sure; but still a chance. If the actor is lucky, smart, and talented, he or she can make it in a comparatively short time. Many stars incorporate themselves into companies, thus obtaining tax advantages as well as exercising more nearly complete control over projects with which they are connected.

With the money comes fame; or, more accurately stated, because of fame the money comes. There is almost no fame in the world equal to that attained by top film, recording, and television stars, but this has its downside, too. It's almost impossible for a "star" to enjoy a quiet family dinner out, visit Disneyland, or just go shopping or have lunch with a friend.

The newspapers often report that celebrities are being stalked or otherwise harassed by obsessed fans. None of the performer unions will give out addresses or telephone numbers—even to other members. Only the phone numbers of agents, answering services, and business managers are given out to callers. If members receive a great number of calls, the unions will notify them that someone is trying to reach them. Some years ago, a law went into effect in California permitting California residents to keep their home addresses private when registering with the Department of Motor Vehicles because it was through that department that an obsessive fan of a television star, then appearing in a popular series, tracked her down and killed her at home.

While fame rarely results in this kind of tragedy, it is often a burdensome inconvenience and responsibility, not nearly as pleasant as the notoriety itself. Most public actions—and many supposedly private ones—are served with breakfast by the newspapers of every major city. Marriage, divorce, romance, sexual orientation, legal problems, finances, and personal affairs become public property. Just how much deference a star owes an adoring but curious and fickle public remains a point of frequent disagreement between stars and the tabloid press or paparazzi. The paparazzi create a major invasion of privacy for celebrities, but there is very little that can be done about this problem. The Internet, too, spreads unflattering photos and unsubstantiated stories or gossip, but this, too, is not illegal.

The fine line between legitimate publicity and tasteless exploitation has been erased in many cases. People in other professions are relatively free to live their lives as they see fit with little fear of public recrimination, simply because their names aren't news. But the well-known performer is constantly exposed to the searchlight of publicity. Even an actor's preference for a political candidate can cause comment and make enemies.

Celebrity and fame have both advantages and disadvantages for performers. Phil Donahue, best remembered as a popular television talk show host, included a chapter on celebrity in his best-selling autobiography. One of the advantages, he humorously noted, was that "with minimal effort, a celebrity . . . could go for weeks without picking up a check." On the one hand, it's nice to be recognized and given special consideration. But on the other, one has absolutely no privacy, and the press and public invade every aspect of one's life. Although a celebrity may fear being recognized and mobbed in public, "a bigger fear," says Donahue, "is *not* being recognized and mobbed, and experiencing the embarrassment of an approach by someone who says, 'I hear you're a very famous person. . . . Who are you?'"

One of the most obvious advantages afforded the successful actor is the freedom from routine. While the study of acting or the repetition of a specific role may be routine, certainly the overall life is not. There is no sitting behind a desk from nine to five. Opportunities for travel are relatively great, and the opportunities for increasing one's overall capabilities are exceptional. Actors are sometimes placed on salary weeks before rehearsals or production begin, to learn new skills such as sign language or horseback riding.

There are other rewards, too, that are more important though seemingly less material. Asked what the theater had given him, the legendary actor and playwright Howard Lindsay answered:

> It has been my education. Where else could I have traveled so far? I have been in the streets of Corinth when Jason and Medea were throwing harsh words at each other. I was at Aulis when the Greek fleet sailed to Troy. I was in Mycenae when Orestes came back to kill his mother, Clytemnestra. I have been in the drawing rooms

of Lady and Lord Windermere of London. And I shouldn't forget to say, I have ridden into western towns with the James Brothers! Where else could I have done things like that?

Personal Requirements

What are the complex personality factors that comprise the actor? Must the actor be an extrovert, continually poised, self-assured, and attractive? Of course—only no one ever is, so neither is the actor. The notion that an extroverted personality is essential to the actor does not necessarily apply to one's personal life. The word "extrovert" brings to mind someone who is perpetually the center of attention at a party; one who talks glibly, seldom at a loss for words. Obviously, not all actors have to be this way. Indeed, some of the most famous and talented stars appear to be quite the opposite, and people who are apparently shy and quiet in a social atmosphere sometimes find the extroverted aspect of their personality at work only on the stage or before a camera. Just as often, the party extrovert may be unable to function in front of a real and paying audience. What is needed then is sufficient personal freedom to act—emancipation from the self-consciousness that destroys an actor's concentration.

A recent survey listed five common "fears" of people in order of importance. Speaking before a public audience ranked number one. Most people are required to do this only occasionally, yet actors build whole careers on this fear-provoking activity.

Nervousness is a problem that must be faced by every performer. I know one world-famous actress who became extremely ill before her entrance each time she opened in a play. But her onstage performance was never affected, or, needless to say, she would not have been a star.

A *New Yorker* magazine cartoon depicts a group of suspects getting ready for the police lineup. One of them says to another, "As many times as I've gone on, I still get butterflies in my stomach."

We smile at the story of the young actress who said to Sarah Bernhardt, "What is this stage fright that I hear so much about? I never have it." Bernhardt answered, "It will come—with talent."

Tennessee Ernie Ford nicely summarized what has come to be known as "stage fright" or "opening night jitters": "The mind is a wonderful thing," he said. "It starts to work the moment we are born, and never stops until we stand up in front of an audience to speak."

The point of these and countless other anecdotes is that nervousness is unavoidable. Whether one is an actor, singer, dancer, announcer, or a guest on a television talk show—it is part and parcel of a public performance. So the problem is not whether an actor will be nervous, but whether the nervousness will hinder the effective performance of the actor's task.

Stage fright does, of course, have real symptoms—perspiration, vomiting, dry throat, palpitations, shaking hands—and there is a definite difference between stage fright and ordinary preperformance anxiety. Diane Nichols, a psychotherapist and clinical social worker who had considerable experience working with performing artists, found that "while anxiety is known to be helpful in creating a great performance, and many actors learn to healthily channel their anxiety and use it to heighten the quality of their performance, many others find their anxiety blocking creativity." Therefore, she says, it is essential that performers "come to grips with the self-defeating state of mind that has caused the debilitating anxiety."

Physical symptoms have to be dealt with, says Ms. Nichols, but:

> . . . equally important is reversing the spiral of negative thinking that causes the performer to define himself as inadequate, and it

is often necessary to uncover whatever unconscious conflicts are at the root of the anxiety. Does the actor suffer from distraction, from a concentration or memory problem? Does he fear disapproval or humiliation? Maybe he's concerned about truly inadequate performing ability or lack of preparation. Or does he fear a loss of love or of success—or is it simply a fear of the fear itself? Perhaps it's anger at an authority figure—parent, agent, director—or even the audience. Often it's a combination of several of these factors.

Al Pacino has said that he finds the challenge of an encounter with the public "scary . . . a walk on the wire."

Ms. Nichols recommends several starting points for resolving this problem. When tension begins building up because of negative thinking, she says, "The first action to take is to smile. To smile without relaxing the body muscles is impossible and, strange as it may seem, changing the pattern of facial muscles sometimes actually effects a change in the emotions." Next, she says, "take two very slow, very deep breaths, which will affect the cardiovascular system and lower the state of psychological arousal."

The idea is not for the anxiety to disappear, Ms. Nichols says, "but for the performer, once back in the driver's seat, to be able to use that anxiety creatively—to be able to channel it constructively in performance-enhancing ways."

Training and technique can help combat stage fright. Concentration on the task (or the objective) of the character the actor is portraying is perhaps the most effective antidote for nervousness. The more one thinks as the character, the less one thinks about oneself, and since nervousness is self-consciousness, the less nervous the actor will be.

Technique, like concentration, also comes with training, working, and appearing on stage before every audience at any opportunity. The more exposure an actor has, the better he or she is able to handle nervousness—not eliminate it, mind you, but cope with it—and often use it to help achieve a peak performance.

If, repeatedly in the same role, the performer is constantly miserable and frightened at the prospect of appearing before an audience or camera, serious thought of an acting career should be abandoned. At best, acting is a tough, demanding business. Who wants to be constantly miserable doing a job that one has to make an extraordinary effort to get?

Physically, there are no strict requirements for an actor's appearance—if there ever were. Unusual physical attractiveness is undoubtedly an asset for young men or women playing romantic roles, but even that requirement is honored as much in the breach as in the observance. Personal magnetism or just being an interesting person is more essential to the career of the well-rounded working actor than stereotyped "attractiveness."

A good memory is vital; so is the ability to take orders, for any production is a ship of which the director is captain, and mutiny is not encouraged. This does not mean that an actor is not expected to bring her or his own interpretation to a role, but the actor must be sufficiently flexible to become part of an integrated unit in relation to the other characters. It is the director's job to see and fuse the production as a whole, to be objective; it is the actor's job to bring interpretation, intelligence, and concentration to the production and to adapt them to the overall requirements of the script. In essence, while the actor is subjective, he or she still must be willing to submerge individual ego for the sake of the play or film as a whole.

On the star level, success traditionally has been equated with an ability to attract customers to the box office or viewers to the television. Obviously, this applies only to the star. Featured players and other performers are engaged because of their proficiency or proven dependability or because their personal qualities relate to the parts they are to fill. But a star's name is expected to sell tickets and/or products, and the star's success and salary are related directly to the amount of money the producers estimate the star can generate.

Ironically, while many actors think of the Broadway stage as the zenith of professional recognition, there are a number of top-ranking Broadway stars whose names mean little in films. Many stage stars whose performances have contributed immensely to the success of a Broadway hit have not been given the opportunity to repeat their role in the motion picture adaptation of the play. With few exceptions, every star of international repute has either appeared in a number of successful motion pictures or headlined a long-running television series.

The success of a project generally is based on having a "star" in the leading role. But there are a number of other important factors, as well: script, timeliness, publicity, critical reviews, audience "word-of-mouth," and—always—luck.

Yet producers, backers, sponsors, networks, and advertising agencies—all the elements that control the purse strings—have a tendency to equate a star's success with the star's ability to attract customers or viewers. This fact is, whether we like it or not, solid proof that acting is a business. The public is notoriously fickle, so "stardom," too, is often fleeting and should not be taken for granted.

Paradoxes of the Business

The paradox of making a business out of an art (and vice versa) is reflected in the entertainment profession as a whole. The entire economic fabric is zany and unpredictable, with only a single factor constant: the need to make a profit on investment.

When business is bad, television or high ticket prices are blamed. Actually, television has had a very considerable impact on theater and films. Why should people pay to see something that doesn't interest them when they can watch something they like for nothing? Today, too, most households have DVDs and cable television and people are able to see popular movies at very low cost. What happens, of course, is that when good films are made, the entire film industry benefits; when good plays are produced on Broadway, theater everywhere is helped.

On Broadway, "marginal" shows, which get good critical reviews but have limited appeal, can seldom survive at the box office. It now costs more than $20 million to put on a Broadway musical: *Beauty and the Beast* cost $15 million, and Disney's *The Lion King* cost $22 million.

Not so many years ago, any play that ran one hundred performances was a success on every level; now a show may run a year and still close without paying back its investment.

Job Opportunities

Actors' employment is a complicated subject, for several reasons. There are three major performer unions: Actors' Equity Association (AEA), the American Federation of Television and Radio Artists (AFTRA), and the Screen Actors Guild (SAG). Each maintains a separate jurisdiction and keeps separate employment statistics on a week-to-week basis, unrelated to other unions' statistics. Also, some performers remain on the unions' rosters even after they become inactive or leave the business. Those people are numbered among the unemployed. The unions can't tell you exactly how many people worked last year; they can tell only how many contracts were signed in their own jurisdictions. Any of its members who are not working under an Equity contract—even if they might be making a movie under SAG's jurisdiction or appearing in a soap opera under an AFTRA contract—are listed by Equity as unemployed.

Published reports that offer statistics to support broad and absolute generalizations are obviously not accurate. Although the greatest problem facing the acting profession is unemployment, the promulgation of such dire figures as gospel tends to downgrade the total employment picture of the average actor.

Still, prospects are not bright. This is true in every field—film, television, or stage—and while it is not news that unemployment is chronic, there actually are more jobs available now than there were many years ago. Films, television (both network and cable), theater (including regional theater), industrial shows, radio, and commercials all offer opportunities for employment. Still, the percentage of working members does not rise proportionately because the unions' membership rolls are larger than they used to be, and competition among the many actors for the relatively few jobs is ever more intense than it was when there were fewer actors. There are more than 120,000 membership cards now outstanding in the performer unions comprising the Associated Actors and Artistes of America (commonly called the Four A's). Actors often belong to more than one union, and, while the total number of individuals who hold membership cards in all the acting unions is not known, we do know how many members each union has. A typical example of the swelling actor ranks is the increase in the membership of Actors' Equity Association, which went from about 14,000 in 1970 to more than 27,000 in 1980 to more than 45,000 in 2004. AFTRA also has grown from 34,000 in 1974 to 70,000 in 1984 to about 80,000 in 2004. Membership in SAG has increased to more than 100,000 in 2004.

The population of the United States grows larger every year and this expansion reflects itself everywhere. Performers wander into the theater in increasing numbers, with or without any talent, so the unions grow willy-nilly. But the sale of additional television sets, for example, will not necessarily mean an increase in the number of actors televised.

U.S. Labor Department studies reveal that the jobs of performing artists tend to be more intermittent than those of other working people; their periods without work are more numerous and longer lasting, and their pay is well below that of other professionals and many other American workers. The data indicate that a successful career in the performing arts requires considerable versatility to move from one artistic discipline to another and, often, from a job as a performer to a job outside the profession, which helps the artist "survive" while waiting for another opportunity as a performer.

It must be stressed that figures gleaned from actors' unions cannot possibly reflect the total earnings of the average actor, because although actors may be employed at other work, they are considered unemployed by the actors' unions unless they are at work in that union's jurisdiction. Of course, the unions' statistics do not reflect money earned from work outside of the performing arts: waiting tables, driving cabs, and so forth.

Suffice it to say, a considerable amount of artistic training and talent is underutilized. An important job consideration for many performers who take temporary work outside the arts is flexibility in hours, so they can continue their careers by attending auditions and making the rounds.

However, despite the bleak employment picture—the surplus of job applicants, the lack of job security, and the uncertainty of financial reward—performers remain strongly committed to their profession.

Adjustment

No matter where the actor works, he or she must adapt; "adjust-ment" is what it's called in the acting profession. Essentially common to all acting, no matter where it is done, is what famed director Elia Kazan called "a sense of truth," making the character believable and acceptable to an audience. However, there are certain differences in technique or execution, and these are peculiar to each medium in which the actor works. These differences demand of the actor facility and adjustment.

The actor on the stage must commit to memory an entire script (often upwards of one hundred pages), must sustain a performance for two or three hours, and must do it eight times a week. If the performance is poor, the actors cannot send the audience out of the theater and begin again. Granted, they usually have three or four weeks of rehearsal to iron out any difficulties, but in the final analysis, once on the stage, the actors must rely on their own abilities.

The same actor working on a film does not labor under all of these disadvantages. There is a microphone to amplify the voice. If one makes a mistake, the scene can be done again; sometimes, various parts of different "takes" are pieced together in the cutting room to capture the best moments of a scene. The actor does not have to learn the whole script at once or deliver it during a single performance.

But in exchange for these seeming props and safety nets, the film makes its own unique demands, so the situation works conversely, too. It is not easy to report for work at 5:00 A.M. and begin in the middle of an emotional scene, and it is often hard to pinpoint the continuity of the story in relation to the actor's character, especially when the last or middle part of a picture is filmed first, as often happens. Many experienced Broadway stars doing their first film have been terrified into near-paralysis by the microphones and cameras. The stage actor in front of a camera for the first time may be somewhat thrown by the necessity of having to "hit marks" (without seeming to notice them) when moving from one place to another within a set. These "marks" are, quite literally, marks on the floor made with tape or chalk, and they are used as distance guides in focusing the camera. The film actor also should have some understanding of the camera and what its lenses do. For example, a person's face on a motion picture screen may be magnified some thirty times, consequently, the stage actor must be able to leave a large theater after projecting her or his voice and emotions to the balcony, and enter the film studio prepared to convey these same emotions by techniques far more subdued. The flicker of an eyelash on the stage will not be noticed; the vitality required on stage becomes grotesque on film. Generally, however, it is easier to cut down than build up. A person who can lift 500 pounds will have no trouble with 250; if 75 pounds is the maximum to which one is accustomed, 100 pounds will surely cause a strain.

Lord Laurence Olivier, who acted both on stage and in films, had this advice in his book, *On Acting*: "If you're having trouble with your relationship with the camera, look to your makeup, gestures and expressions; look to your eyes; look within yourself. And get your feeling and mood right. If all else fails, talk to the director."

While dramatic television shows today are made on tape or film, the early days of television saw mostly live performances. These made incredible demands on the actor, for they required combined knowledge of both stage and film techniques and the most rigorous discipline required by either of them. Not only did the actor have to understand and adjust a performance to the placement of lights, microphones, cameras, cables, and a virtual circus of behind-the-camera distractions, he or she also had to commit to memory the entire script in a very short period of rehearsal time and work with the certain knowledge that if the performance wasn't good the first time, there was no second take. In addition, live television required that an actor be concerned with such matters as changing costumes quickly (perhaps during a commercial), racing across the stage to a different set, and then delivering a convincing love scene. In view of all this, it is really something of a wonder that any good performances were seen at all on live dramatic television. And many were.

Trends

One trend that is not exactly new is taking off one's clothes. The Broadway plays *Hair* and *Oh, Calcutta!* started it on stage, and the subsequent rush to disrobe still has many actors exposed and shivering. Although some appear to take easily to the trend, it has not proven to be the route to lasting stardom.

Actors' Equity Association has found it necessary to adopt a nudity code to protect its members. The code stipulates that no nudity is permitted at interviews, or until after the actor has been auditioned. Nudity at auditions is permitted only when an official union representative and duly authorized members of the production team are present. No actor is required to appear nude in a production unless he or she has been advised and gives written consent by the time of signing the contract. Actors are not required to pose for nude photographs or to appear nude for any motion picture filming, videotaping, or other forms of visual recording without written consent. No photograph in which an actor appears nude may be used in any way without the written consent of each actor appearing in the photograph, and even then, the request to use the photograph must specify the use to be made of the photo. No actor is required, while nude, to mix with the audience or to leave the stage or performing area, and no member of the audience is permitted to enter the stage, performance area, or backstage while any actor is nude.

Although these rules are specifically for members of Actors' Equity Association, it would be wise for all performers to be very clear on the circumstances before agreeing to disrobe at any time.

Movies, of course, have had to adapt a rating system as nudity—and offensive language—have become almost commonplace. Cable television has a no-holds-barred policy.

Perhaps from our standpoint, a more appropriate definition of a "trend" would be a development that has an impact on potential employment for the actor.

Broadway remains the theatrical capital of the country, but there is no question that American theater has diversified. Jerome Lawrence, noted playwright (*Inherit the Wind*, *Auntie Mame*) feels that "a lot of theater outside New York is better than Broadway. Some of it is sloppy and screwy, but some of it is great. American theater shouldn't be confined to a few blocks in Manhattan. Plays should be written and performed elsewhere—not before Broadway, but instead of Broadway."

Veteran actor Eli Wallach told a meeting of actors that "the theater has essentially moved off-Broadway, but there are wonderful productions going on with wonderful actors. There's no difference between that and Broadway." He also told the story of playing Mr. Freeze on an episode of *Batman* when it was a television series in 1967. Although a well-known performer at the time, he was paid $350 for a half-hour show. In 1996, Arnold Schwarzenegger was paid $22 million to play Mr. Freeze in *Batman*, the film.

For the actor, the proliferation of theaters away from the mainstream offers increased opportunities to escape casting stereotypes and to create new roles and innovative theater. Colleges and universities also are affiliating with professional theater groups, giving increased opportunities to students and professional actors.

In New York, there was only the Broadway theater. Then, as production costs mounted and astronomic theater rentals and limited theater availabilities drove all but the most successful (and commercial) plays to early closings, the off-Broadway theater emerged and offered some of the most interesting and worthwhile plays to audiences for a fraction of the cost of a Broadway ticket. Stars such as Frank Langella, Al Pacino, and Dustin Hoffman first achieved recognition in off-Broadway productions.

But soon off-Broadway became as expensive to produce and see as Broadway had been years before; so now we have off-off Broadway. It is in this area that the little theater groups and workshops are finding audiences. Many off-off Broadway productions are not union; many of them don't pay the performers. But these workshops are places to be seen, and since the number of summer theaters—which used to serve as the crucible for developing an actor's talents—has declined, aspiring actors must use every available showcase until their careers get off the ground.

It is in these venues that the actor has a chance to work with fledgling directors, writers, designers, and other technicians. Then, if an actor "makes it," he or she has developed a reservoir of friends to call upon and to recommend to directors and producers.

There are other new developing fields opening up for talented actors as well. Cable television, commercials, infomercials, voice-overs, dubbing, and even recording books on tape are all of potential significance to actors. With the continued introduction of new technologies, who knows what the future will bring for performers as well as for society as a whole? In the field of electronic entertainment, the possibilities are endless. Anything that is telecast or originates on film can potentially be collected by private individuals. The performers' unions have been alert to these developments and are aware of the tremendous potential for exploitation of the actor or musician. It is easy to imagine how one performance seen over and over and over again would lead to unemployment for the artists and large profits for the companies duplicating their performances.

The Effects of Emerging Technologies

Technology is changing so rapidly it is difficult to keep up with the new developments, and what we talk about now might well be obsolete or gone before this ink is dry.

Unfortunately, opportunities for performers are not keeping pace with the advances in technology. In fact, the new technologies are causing problems for performers in terms of unauthorized duplication of their work—both audio and video—which, in turn, robs them of employment opportunities.

Naturally, the performer unions are concerned with problems caused by home recording and duplicating, and although it has been said that imitation is the highest form of flattery, that very imitation often prevents a person from being paid for her or his labor.

Millions of people are making free copies of music CDs and DVDs on their computers. Others are taping valuable television programs or copying prerecorded videos for friends and neighbors. Performers are not paid for these copies of their work, and it has been estimated that the recording industry loses more than $1 billion in sales each year from such practices.

The American Federation of Television and Radio Artists (AFTRA), the Screen Actors Guild (SAG), and the Musicians' Union especially are extremely concerned over piracy—the duplication and electronic transmission of a performance.

AFTRA is also concerned with voice tracking—replacing live local announcers with recorded tracks that can serve many markets. Obviously, this impacts on the employment of local talent.

Then there is the technology that allows film or videotape to reproduce the human form, creating a "crowd" digitally, where before, hundreds of extras needed to be hired.

Not to be forgotten is the increase in "reality" television shows—using real people instead of actors in productions. As ratings for these shows go up, there are fewer "scripted" shows being produced and fewer professional actors being hired. Obviously, television producers and networks welcome the success of these reality shows as they are relatively inexpensive to produce.

Rising costs and the constant attention to the "bottom line" of profits affect every business. In theater, Actors' Equity recently had to face the proliferation of non-union touring shows. Producers were taking popular Broadway shows out on the road to theaters across the country, using nonprofessional and less-expensive actors. Equity faced this problem in its recent contract negotiations, created a lower salary scale to be competitive, and adopted the slogan, "If it's not Equity, it's not Broadway," so that audiences around the country will learn the difference. While young actors might find non-union touring attractive, it offers substandard salaries and minimum fringe benefits.

Cable television originated in the late 1940s as a means of delivering an acceptable television signal to rural areas that could not receive a clear signal off the air. Today, so many of the cable television channels currently operating are local access stations, catering to a wide range of civic interests and group discussions, that despite all the hoopla that has attended their emergence, they offer scant opportunity for performers. Present local cable operations are concerned primarily with filling time, and they fill it with virtually anything available. Certainly they don't feature performances by actors, singers, or dancers. The big cable networks, on the other hand, fill much of their time with movies, sports broadcasts, or news.

Although the performer unions have negotiated additional payment when newer movies or television programs are sold to cable, the additional income generated by these agreements has not been significant.

As all of the performer unions wrestle with the problems caused by new technologies and the protection of "intellectual property," several years ago, AFTRA established its first contract covering work in interactive media, including work in videogames and interactive movies. The number of companies and producers using the agreement increases every year.

Technology also affects the way performers look for work. The Internet and e-mail have changed the world—and that includes the entertainment industry. The Internet can be a valuable research and networking tool. In addition, there is a major service available to actors—for a subscription fee.

Breakdown Services, Ltd., is the communications network and casting system that provides synopses of scripts to agents and casting directors, as well as actors, for the purpose of casting. Offices are located in Los Angeles, New York, and Vancouver, with sister companies in Toronto, London, and Sydney. A "breakdown" is a description of all the speaking and nonspeaking parts, with information on the size of each role and where the character first appears in the script. Talent representatives are able to instantly view the breakdowns and submit their clients' pictures, résumés, and videos via the Breakdown website to casting directors.

Script pages, called "sides," are available through the Breakdown Services website at showfax.com.

For complete information on Breakdown Services, visit the website at breakdownservices.com.

2

GETTING STARTED

IT HAS BEEN said that performers spend more time looking for work than actually working. Even for successful performers, there is always the need for a new movie, new television show, or new Broadway production—in short, a new job. Many television series have run for years, as have Broadway shows, but at the end of the run, it's always back to square one—looking for that next job.

When interviewed for *Back Stage West*, the Hollywood casting newspaper, one casting director for a hit television series told a story that illustrates this. He was working with a prominent actor who had been nominated for an Oscar, was starring in a hit play, and had received wonderful reviews; yet he felt he needed to get a new agent. "Some things never change," the casting director said, noting that "there are great and glorious things and rewards to acting, but it's also a very tough lifestyle."

Another film star, whose career spanned four decades, told me that after winning an Oscar for his performance in a hit movie, he didn't get offered another script for two years.

31

Tony Award–winning actor Frank Langella, in an article for the *New York Times*, spoke of the "demon seesaw actors ride." He told of a veteran character actor who had told him that he is so excited when a job comes to a close that he takes himself and his family on vacation and for a few days is in bliss. And then, every time the phone rings, he runs "like an old fool" to catch it, saying "Oh, God, please don't hang up. I hope it's work." So for the newcomer and veteran alike, there is always the process of getting started.

In acting, as in any other extremely competitive situation, certain basic criteria apply. Known as the "five D's," these are: desire, drive, determination, dedication, and discipline. It is necessary to possess all of these qualities in large quantities if one is to succeed as an actor.

What this really means is that a person planning a career as an actor has to want that career more than anything in the world and be willing to make considerable sacrifices to achieve this goal. This degree of commitment to a career can be a source of problems, unless everyone involved understands and is able to support the commitment. Entire lives are spent getting and keeping started. The big question is, "How do you do it?"

Let's begin with a dialogue between the former star of a daytime television series and Theodore Bikel, the prominent entertainer, star of *Fiddler on the Roof*, and former president of Actors' Equity. Here are some excerpts from that conversation:

Q. How does one become a "professional"?

A. By behaving like a professional. One must work, study, and starve like a professional. Performing requires great discipline. A professional must be on time and feel on time.

Q. How does a young person know whether to become a performer?

A. You should become a performer if you can't live without performing, if you would die spiritually if you didn't become a performer, and if you would be happy with nothing else.

Q. Should a young actor go to New York or California or stay home to get started?

A. Today, it is possible to stay home. The theater has gone where the people are. Major casting still is done in the large production centers, but smaller parts are cast from local talent.

Q. Should an actor get an agent or manager early in her or his career?

A. An agent usually doesn't get an actor a job; once an actor has the job, the agent negotiates the terms. Actors have to hustle for themselves. Agents are franchised by the unions; managers are not recognized officially by anyone. A newcomer should be careful about signing with managers.

In short, said Mr. Bikel, there are "no shortcuts" to becoming an actor. Training, working, and working-to-find-work are what count.

Several prominent members were asked by *AFTRA Magazine*, the official publication of the American Federation of Television and Radio Artists, to offer some advice to people just starting out in their careers. Here's what they had to say:

Anne Archer, film (*Fatal Attraction*) and television star:

> When you are a young actor getting started—study, study, study! Do theater, especially in New York. Learn how to keep in friendly

positive communication with your agent, always telling him or her the good news—something positive someone said, a great project you heard about, et cetera. Make him or her feel like you're a team. Be helpful; take responsibility for creating a warm and helpful relationship with your agent.

Ed Bradley, news broadcaster (*60 Minutes*):

What worked for me was hard work. Being the first one in, the last to leave—looking for something else, something more to do. I'd say, "If this is my task, what else can I do?" For example, when I started in radio, I was ostensibly a disc jockey. That was not all I wanted to do. So I looked for other things to do as well. But you know, it was fun. I enjoyed it. I did news, I did sports, I did play-by-play of basketball games; I did anything I could to get on the air. So you try to expand your horizon to see how much you can do.

Jay Leno, comedian and star of *The Tonight Show*:

The real trick is to try to get in as much stage time as you can—any place, any time. Doing comedy is like working out with weights—you have to do it every day or you will atrophy. Quit that second job as soon as you can and stay with show business. I've always felt that the worst thing for a show business career is to make $30,000 a year doing something else. You get to the point where you say, "I don't want to go to that audition; the job doesn't pay anything." You have to do it because you like doing it. And you have to try to live on what you make as a performer.

The late actor Christopher Reeve (*Superman*), in *Equity News*, the official publication of Actors' Equity Association:

I think the more time you can build up playing important roles, wherever, the better. I would think it's better to get to play Edmund in *Long Day's Journey into Night* at even a non-Equity theater. It's better to play parts. If somebody can actually show up on a Friday night, sit there, and see you being good in something—that is the best.

Uta Hagen, actress and teacher, in her book, *A Challenge for the Actor*:

> I believe that when you have achieved great skill, a point of view, and the power to communicate, an audience no matter how small, will reward you with the respect that makes it all worthwhile. If you are willing to make a true commitment to the making of theater art, like a dedicated priest or nun, you will have to accept the likelihood of poverty in exchange for inner riches. It is the only trade-off you can hope for.

Frank Langella, actor:

> I would never discourage anybody, ever. Never give up and never give in. It doesn't matter what the odds are. You really can do whatever you want to do, and if you don't succeed it's because you didn't try hard enough. I think it's much better to go down in flames.

A senior vice president of talent and casting at ABC Entertainment, for readers of *Back Stage West*:

> You have to believe completely that absolutely anything is possible in this world. I believe with all my heart that people who are talented will eventually succeed no matter how long it takes. So take the day as it comes and do the best you can. I remember when I had to do a job search, I made a list of all the people I was going to contact to help me get a job, and every day I took at least one action to advance my goal.

A prominent casting director said:

> A true actor must love acting above all else. If you love acting, you'll find a place to act—even in a park or a street corner. And

the fact that you get paid to do what you love to do is the icing on the cake.

Morgan Freeman, three-time Academy Award nominee:

The only advice I have for any actor is keep acting. Just keep working. And keep your mind on what you want. It's bound to happen if you keep working. One thing leads to another and if you have a goal, you're bound to reach it—if you just keep going.

Michael Keaton, actor (*Batman*):

As for acting, I'd urge anyone interested in the profession to keep doing it. Any time you can get on the stage in front of people—or not in front of people—just say words off a script. Just talk. Express yourself. Start from that. Start from the basics and keep on doing it. And do it for the right reasons. Do it because you kind of need to do it, or really want to do it.

Working at Working

Even with all the luck and talent in the world, success at acting (and by "success" I mean "finding work," not "becoming a star") depends on training and commitment.

You must be the one to beat the bushes on your own behalf. You will make mistakes. You will be told you are too young, too old, too pretty, too thin, not pretty enough, too handsome, too American, or "not what the director has in mind." You will be frustrated to the point of quitting the business, and perhaps you ought to quit. You will be stunned to discover (if ever you do) that the world is not waiting for you to become a star. Nobody but you cares.

Actors also need to understand that they can't do everything, especially under the microscope vision of a camera. They've got to realize that physical things come very much into bearing—such things as family relationships required by the script and basic qualities in the actor or actress that are compatible with the character.

Anne Archer told *AFTRA Magazine* that:

> All actors experience rejection throughout their careers. Even as you become a major star, especially for women, you continue to have to fight for roles, and continue to be rejected. There are not enough good roles to go around, so there are always those who lose out. It is a part of being a performer. You must simply put it behind you and go on. Whether it is a meeting or an audition you are facing, it is important to view that meeting or audition as an end in itself. If it goes well, consider the job done. Having a number of these successes puts one in the frame of mind to eventually get the job. Work in a class, do a play, take voice lessons, write, et cetera—whatever keeps the creative flow going. Eventually, the work comes.

A working actor has said:

> An actor and a salesman are the two professions that you get the most rejection in. But an actor is rejected for who he is. It's very difficult in that sense. Once you learn how to play the game, it gets easier. Once you get hit on the head a hundred times with a hammer, it doesn't hurt anymore. You learn that's your job and you are always putting yourself out there and asking "What do you think?"

Swoosie Kurtz, a popular stage and television actress who has been nominated for many awards, told a meeting of Actors' Equity:

> I'm sure that you look at me and probably think, "She's got it made; she's got all the answers; she's nominated for a Tony . . ." But I am going to tell you, you may think as you go on it gets easier, and in some ways it does. Instead of having to go over to the casting office to look at the sides and read (and P.S. they won't give you the whole script and you don't know what it's about and you have to go in blind), now they deliver the script to me. But it

doesn't mean that I have any larger chance of getting the role. You gotta roll with the punches.

It's not easy. They always tell you, "Don't take it personally; it's not about you." Well, we are our own instrument. If you are selling dresses and someone doesn't buy the dress you can say, they didn't like the dress, it doesn't really reflect on you. But we are our own body's voice, so when they cast somebody else and you know, it hurts. You can't help but think it's about you; they like the other person better. I think you have to be really strong in knowing your own identity and believing in yourself.

Even if and when you become established in the profession, when each engagement ends, the perpetual task of job-hunting begins again. Indeed, the working actor, realizing that her or his current employment is of limited duration, often performs one task while hunting for the next. The process never ends.

Job Hunting

For the novice who has never had a job before, the job of getting a job is harder. What do you do first? How do you find out where the jobs are? Well, you read, you ask, you listen. You read the trade papers of the acting business, many of which contain some casting information. Among these are the weekly *Variety*, *Back Stage*, and *Ross Reports*, published in New York. *Daily Variety*, *Hollywood Reporter*, and *Back Stage West* are the leading trade papers published in Los Angeles. The theatrical columns of the daily newspapers sometimes announce production plans in advance of actual casting. For example, if a paper carries an item saying that a producer plans to do a play that will be adapted from a book, it is wise to read the book. If there's a character that you think you're right for, you'll know what you're talking about when you visit the office to ask for an interview.

Next you "make the rounds." Making the rounds is merely the process of going from office to office looking for work. It is a dismal business, discouraging and filled with rejection. Most of the people you want to see do not want to see you, especially if you're not appearing in anything where they can see your work. Actors make the rounds of producers' offices and offices of the casting directors who work for the advertising agencies that produce television programs or commercials—in short, everyone and anyone remotely able to hire or recommend you for a job. This is especially true in New York. In Hollywood, you need an agent for virtually everything; in New York, it is not the least bit out of order to make the rounds yourself. Some agents set aside specific hours for seeing actors and some don't see them at all, preferring to collect photos and résumés and then call the actor if something comes up. It's a good idea to check on a specific agent's policy before visiting the office. This information is carried in some of the trade papers, and specifically in *Ross Reports*, which also gives specific information on the areas in which a particular agent is active (television, films, stage) and the kinds of clients represented (children, no children).

It is also important to be organized when making the rounds. Cabs are expensive, buses aren't always prompt, and walking can be exhausting. Therefore, a simple geographic breakdown will help save time and energy. Plan to cover one section or block, or even just one building at a time. This simple discipline may prove very helpful.

Jackson Beck, a well-known and highly successful radio and commercial voice-over talent, began his career in 1930. Once he made up his mind to be a performer, he took a map of New York City and marked the locations of all the advertising agencies, networks, agents, and others who could provide him with employment;

then he divided the city into five-block squares. Each day, he knocked on doors within a particular square and made notes about the people he talked with and what they said. After a couple of months, he got an agent to represent him and landed his first job. This same procedure is still a good idea.

If an agent sends you for an interview, in all likelihood you are being submitted for a particular part. Even when visiting an office on your own, it is better to have something specific in mind—a role that you know the office is trying to cast and for which you think you are right. Try to have some kind of objectivity about yourself. If you are a twenty-two-year-old woman on the slim side, don't try to convince a casting director that you would be wonderful as the fat grandmother in a Broadway play just because you played a grandmother in college. That's fine for college. For Broadway, they'll get someone who looks the part.

It's not always possible to have a specific part in mind when making rounds; sometimes you are just trying to get acquainted with the people at the offices. But, needless to say, the more you have read or heard about a producer's plans, the better off you are.

One employment opportunity that is often not exploited sufficiently is the play about to go on the road. Often, the Broadway cast is unwilling to accompany a show after it closes in New York; sometimes, even if a show isn't closing, a second or third road production is planned. The trade papers contain announcements of pending touring companies, and if you see every play you can (buy the cheapest seats, but go!) you will know which ones have roles for which you could logically be considered.

When you read of a show going on the road and know there is a part in it for you, visit not only the producer's offices, but also the stage manager backstage. Give the stage manager your picture and résumé. The best time to do this is either directly after a performance or when the stage manager enters the theater about forty-five minutes before the performance starts. Simply tell the doorman at the stage entrance that you want to see the stage manager and then wait. Never drop in while the curtain is up or during the half hour before the play starts. It is then that the stage manager is busiest, and your lack of knowledge or consideration will not be appreciated.

Many professional actors got their first jobs in summer stock or regional theater. By scanning every available trade publication beginning in March, you can get a fairly good idea of upcoming summer stock activity. Start then to write letters, or if you are close enough, make phone calls or personal contacts to determine the possibility of your joining the company. Stock managers usually seek good acting talent geographically close, because they save money by not having to transport actors from Chicago, New York, or Hollywood.

Regional theaters have been established in many cities. The Arena Stage of Washington, D.C.; American Conservatory Theater of San Francisco; the Cleveland Playhouse; the Hartford Stage Company; and the Guthrie Theater of Minneapolis are but a few of the more prominent examples of successful regional theaters. It may be very valuable to scout the regional professional theaters nearest your home to see if you can get a position "apprenticing" with one of them—even if it means not making any money at first.

Dinner theaters are also good prospects, and they should be scouted avidly. But no matter where you try, you are better off if you can display some familiarity with an organization's work before asking it to find a spot for you.

Television soap operas are another good and lucrative training ground. Many stars, including Demi Moore, Alec Baldwin, Kevin

Bacon, Christopher Reeve, Tom Selleck, and Meg Ryan started on the soaps.

As far as breaking into television broadcasting is concerned, you're far more likely to persuade a small station in Omaha that it needs an announcer than to find NBC-TV in New York waiting for you to walk through the door.

No matter what kind of job you're looking for, there is no question that the unknown actor represented by a reputable agent has the edge over another unknown actor who walks in off the street. (This does not apply to chorus singers and dancers, who do not work through agents.) In the first place, the person sent by an agent, whose business it is to sell talent, will have a definite appointment to see a particular person and will get in to see that person. Also, when you are sent by an agent, there is a clear implication that the agent knows your work and recommends it. That is one reason why getting the right agent is sometimes harder than finding a job. Also, if you don't get the part for which you've been sent, a good agent can more often find out the real reason for your rejection—something you are unlikely to learn by yourself.

Usually, you will find that a reputable agent will not submit you for a job without having seen your work. Therefore, it is necessary to find some kind of "showcase" in which you can be seen; in New York, most often these showcases are either professional off-Broadway stage productions or non-Equity shows, staged as workshops or under nonprofessional auspices. Since you won't be working in a nonprofessional production if you are an Equity member, and since parts in professional off-Broadway shows are almost as hard to get as parts on Broadway or in television, it may be to your advantage not to join a union too soon so that you can be free to act wherever and whenever the opportunity occurs. While it is true that your chances of playing a part in summer stock or regional theater are better than they are in New York or Los Angeles, few agents are willing to trek to the hinterlands just to see you perform. They have enough trouble finding jobs for the clients they already have.

Once you get a job in a showcase production, it is your additional responsibility to get every agent or casting director you can possibly persuade to see you. This is not as easy as it seems, and their reluctance to "discover" you may come as a shock. Most will profess to be vitally interested in new talent because, basically, they are decent people who don't want to hurt your feelings.

Once you're in a showcase—one that you honestly believe shows off your abilities to good advantage—you are ready to approach the agents and casting directors. These people should not be expected to pay for their own tickets, especially if you have asked them to view your show. You have to arrange for their tickets. (A *pair* of tickets is usually in order, not just one.) You can take comfort from the fact that everybody else appearing with you in the production will also want to be seen by these people, and if the management of the theater does not sufficiently understand how important it is to set aside a few seats for the use of actors, the rest of the cast can chip in and purchase the tickets together. After all, they have as much to gain as you do.

In Hollywood, too, theatrical (stage) showcases are the main avenues of exposure for unknown actors. There are many little theaters in the Los Angeles area, known as "ninety-nine-seat waiver theaters," and they are good places to be seen. Equity has created special contracts for these productions, and its West Coast office spends a lot of time administering them. Those theaters with fewer than ninety-nine seats can employ anybody they wish, without regard to a performer's union affiliation. So in Los Angeles, as in New York, the showcase theater is a good bet. It is also one of the few places left where one can learn and make mistakes without permanently disastrous results to a career. Many actors work in these small theaters, hoping to be seen by film and television casting directors and producers.

It is much harder to make the rounds for films and television in Hollywood without an agent. In New York, many actors find their own jobs, especially those who work for the unions' minimum salaries. In Hollywood, usually you need an agent, since you cannot even get through a studio gate without an appointment. But always remember: the agent doesn't get you a job. He or she gets you an audition, but you have to get the job yourself.

In this discussion, we have been concentrating on the main production centers, New York and Hollywood. Of course, it is possible, and some distinguished people think it is preferable, to join the acting profession without ever leaving home.

The Paperwork

Paperwork is an essential part of making the rounds; and there is a lot of it. Beginning actors—whether looking for work on stage, screen, or television—must practically run an office to sell themselves properly, for in most cases, without strong aid from an agent, actors can only succeed in getting into offices by sending in some paper first. The mail carrier can get in where the actor is refused. The "three P's" apply to this aspect of the job search: patience, persistence, and postage.

Did you ever stop to realize what happens when an office receives fifty to one hundred mailings from actors in a single day? You must distribute pictures, résumés, and letters—but whether they will work to your benefit or end up in the wastebasket is something else again. Obviously your mailings and deliveries must be as effective as possible, for not only is their preparation time consuming, but they are expensive as well. Here are several useful hints for actors to keep in mind when looking for work:

• Every mailing should have your name, address, and phone number clearly printed on each piece of paper you submit. This goes for photographs, résumés, pieces of notepaper, clippings, or programs.

Except in rare cases, a complicated stack of reading materials is a pure waste when sent to a casting director. Sending a program might prove you were in a show, but a statement on your résumé is easy to check and easier to file. The fewer words you send, the more chance every word will be read. If you must send more than one item in an envelope, be careful to attach all the pieces so that the person opening the envelope cannot avoid removing the entire contents at once. A piece of paper left unnoticed in a discarded envelope does you no good.

• Limit your résumé to a single page, with your experience grouped under appropriate headings, such as "Broadway," "Off-Broadway," "Commercials," "Films," "Television."

The most important items in a résumé are vital statistics (height, weight, color of eyes and hair), contact information, and your professional engagements. Experience in school, community, or amateur theater is helpful if that's all you've had, but once you have a few professional engagements, be certain they hit the reader's eye first.

Then it's time to reduce preprofessional experience to a simple sentence or paragraph, such as "five years' experience acting and stage managing in community theater," or perhaps a succinct listing under "Training." Include your height, weight, and the age range you can competently portray; special abilities such as dancing, singing, dialects, and so forth; and your union affiliations. When you make the rounds, don't wait to write your particulars in each office. Be prepared simply to hand over the material and make a graceful exit before you wear out your welcome.

Make your résumé simple, direct, and short. Above all, be honest. Omit unimportant details so that the reader's attention is taken only by the items that will strongly influence your being hired. For Broadway experience, the titles of the plays are enough. For stock, the names of the theaters and one or two titles tell a great deal. A long list of the roles played is rarely more than skimmed over. Leave something for your interviewer to ask you when you meet in person. Don't mention something in which you know you weren't very good. Sometimes, by being too complete and specific, you place your qualifications within narrow confines and lose out on an interview. Say too much and there's no reason for them to find out anything more about you.

• Attach your résumé firmly to the reverse side of your photograph. A résumé carefully glued, taped, stapled, or actually printed directly on the reverse side of a picture will never get separated from that picture in an overstuffed file. A résumé by itself is worthless and usually gets thrown out; a picture without a résumé is not worth much more. Most casting files are set up for photos or composites printed eight inches across and ten inches down because that is the size of the majority of pictures the producer receives. If yours has the longer measurement across, someone going through the file quickly may not stop to turn the entire stack sideways to get a good look at you. If your photograph is too small, it may fall to the bottom of the file and be unnoticed or lost completely. If your photograph is too large, it may not get into the file at all. If your résumé is larger than your photograph, the edges get torn, curled, or otherwise ruined—again finding the attention of the nearest wastepaper basket. A standard piece of typing paper may look the same size as the standard photo, but it is usually half an inch wider and an inch longer. Cut it down!

• Try to select one good unretouched picture that shows your personality as well as your features. If you need more than one picture to advertise yourself, consider a composite instead of separate photos.

If you send more than one picture, staple them so that they stay together in a file, but put your name, address, and phone number on each, just to be safe. However, you can get a composite printed in quantity for little additional expense with two, three, or more pictures on one page. These composites usually are more useful for seeking work in commercials. Seldom are they an advantage for theatrical casting. They should be used only when the added pictures really show a contrasting (and legitimate) characteristic. Most people can make a variety of grimaces without proving the existence of talent. Producers and directors usually have enough intelligence to realize that the actor who is photographed smiling is capable of appearing without the smile, if called upon to do so. You can also credit most directors with the intelligence to know that an actor can change hairstyle (and color).

Character actors might benefit from showing a variety of pictures, or a bald man might show himself with and without a toupee, but before you go to that trouble, ask yourself if the photos really show an unexpected contrast. Is one photo obviously much older than the other (and therefore valueless)? Is the contrast legitimately useful, or merely a caricature? Will the director or producer divine more about your talents because there are two pictures instead of one?

• Don't send matte photos. Glossies are usually cheaper and will do the job.

• Don't send a picture that doesn't look like you or that you can't make yourself look like. A beautiful and flattering picture may be fine on top of a piano in your mother's living room, but if a photograph gets you an interview and you come in looking like another person, you're wasting your interviewer's time and your own. On the other side of the coin, the interviewer may be looking for someone who looks the way you really look—perhaps not as glamorous as you'd wish, but nevertheless, the real you—and your picture may be bypassed as not the right type. A picture taken in your past may remind you of more enjoyable days, but it probably won't help get your name on a contract.

What about selecting a photographer? Every actor needs good professional photographs, and there are hundreds of photographers available. Be cautious, however. It is wise to select a photographer carefully and to know how much you need and what you may reasonably pay. Before selecting a photographer, check out the ads in the trade publications, ask your coach or teacher for advice, ask your friends, and look for pictures you like and ask who took them. Look at samples of work. It is important to use someone whose work pleases you and with whom you feel comfortable and at ease. Relaxation is a key element in a professionally useful picture. Then work out the arrangements beforehand. What is the cost? Who keeps the negatives? Do you get to choose enlargements from contact prints, and how many enlargements do you get? How much time and film will be used? Where will the session take place? How long must you wait for your photo session? What guarantees, if any, will you get? How long will it be before you get your pictures? When must payment be made? Remember, this is an extremely competitive field, and you may not receive every advantage a photographer is willing to grant if you do not ask for it.

• If you send a fancy mailing piece, plan it for the file where you hope it will be kept. Occasionally, you might accomplish something special that you want to bring vividly to the attention of the agent, casting director, or producer—perhaps great personal notices in an unusual role. In this case, consider sending copies of your notices only if the city or the critic is well known and the notices are good. If you've played in a small town, the local paper's review will not necessarily attest to professional standards of performance. If the *New York Times* says merely that you're "charming," you might pass out cigars, but don't pass out the notice. Carefully consider whether what you submit will really demonstrate professional caliber.

• Don't send any material through the mail that you expect to have returned, unless you enclose a stamped, self-addressed envelope. Even if you do this, you're at the mercy of the efficiency of the office secretary. Besides, any material you send may do its best work weeks or months after it reaches the office. If you send a stamped postcard for a reply, that may be helpful. But don't feel resentful if you never get the card back. The producer may not be able to see you and may be too swamped to send even the simplest reply. If you don't get an answer, try having some compassion for the office that receives enormous loads of mail. Whenever possible, address your mailing to a specific person. If you take enough time to send a letter and a first-class postage stamp, you should at least know to whom you're sending it.

• Take all casting "tips" (published or verbal) with a grain of salt. When a publication that advises actors on casting information carries a misstatement, hundreds of actors may deluge an unsuspecting office with visits and phone calls. This might be flattering to the publication, but it doesn't make the printed word correct. No matter how polite the secretary tries to be, there is often an actor who insists that he or she is being given an unfair brush-off. Because it was published, the actor thinks it must be reliable. When an actor is nasty to a secretary, nothing is accomplished.

Publications, tips, suggestions from friends, and all manner of leads are important and helpful. But remember the possibility that the tip is wrong. When it's right, be happy. When it's wrong, be philosophical.

• If you belong to a union, be certain that it always has your correct address and numbers for your phone, cell, and beeper. Most actors would be surprised to know that hours are sometimes spent in offices trying to track down an actor whom someone remembers and is anxious to reach. I know one particular case where an office tried desperately to reach an actor for a leading role and couldn't find him. A year later, when the road company was being cast, the actor turned up asking for the part. He got the part in the road company, but no one will ever know what he missed the year before on Broadway.

The membership departments of AFTRA, SAG, and Equity constantly receive phone calls from production offices asking for members' addresses. They will give out numbers of agents, business managers, or answering services, but not personal information. This is a valuable service to all performers and is supported by their dues.

• A telephone number that will always be answered during business hours should be part of your basic professional equipment. It is vital that you be reachable by phone at all times. All the preceding information is useless if the producer can't get in touch with you once the decision has been made to see you. If you live at home and someone will always be there to take messages graciously and get the complete message, that's fine. But if the phone is covered only at irregular intervals, or if the person who answers is short-tempered, hard of hearing, has difficulty speaking English, or has any other problem taking messages, invest in a cell phone or beeper. This goes for hotel or apartment switchboards also, when the service is undependable. An electronic answering device on your telephone also can be used. But be sure you have a way of checking its messages at regular intervals. A brief straightforward message is best. Stay away from "cutesy," overlong messages. Prospective employers don't have the time to listen to them and may be annoyed by having to listen to a lot of talk, music, and sound effects before being able to leave a message.

• Whatever you do to reach your customer, use good taste. Sometimes desperation pushes people to use tasteless or even fraudulent means to gain attention. Occasionally, a gimmicky publicity campaign will skyrocket someone of questionable talent to fame. However, instances of such success are rare, and we always hope that "talent will out."

There are dozens of valueless crutches that a desperate aspirant will try. For example, a lie on a résumé is often found out. Another tactic that surprises me is the phone call made to a producer or director long after office hours. When a producer's apartment or home serves also as an office, respect his or her privacy. Don't phone after seven o'clock. Every once in a while I'll hear a producer say, "What are actors coming to these days? I got a call in the middle of the night from someone asking for an interview!" This happens more often than you'd think. Even when you're answering a producer's message to return a call, don't call after seven o'clock.

Don't misuse the custom of writing "personal" on the outside of an envelope. Although it has personal importance to you, it is not "personal" to the producer or director. If the job of a secretary or assistant is to open and read mail, this is being done by order of the producer. You gain nothing by misrepresentation, except a lack of respect.

The Personal Interview

If you have done all the necessary paperwork and have also followed up your résumé with personal visits (a telephone call is usually a waste of time), you are bound to be seen sooner or later. The casting director for one of theater's most active producers recently told me that if a person keeps coming back week after week, and if the person isn't "some kind of eccentric," eventually she will see her or him, because she is curious about anyone "who has that much persistence." Or sometimes, she will see the actor "just to get rid of him." Doubtless, those are not the reasons why you want to be seen, but at least you'll eventually get past the receptionist and into the inner office.

When you do get in, how should you act? Like yourself, unless you wish to attract attention by virtue of your eccentricity—which doesn't pay off in the long run.

The biggest complaints from casting directors are:

- Regional dialects: "If I want a Brooklyn or Southern accent, I'll hire an actress with good speech who can do dialects," said one television casting director.
- Picture doesn't look like the person (too old, too young, too glamorous, too retouched).
- Sloppy or inappropriate dress (women dressing too sexily, too much makeup; men wearing blue jeans or tennis shoes).
- Actors who lie about their abilities or talents (i.e., they tell the casting director of a Western television series that they can ride horseback, then show up on the set not knowing which end of the horse is the front).

It is best to be natural. There is such a short time in which to make an impression. But in any case, to leave the office having created the feeling that you are a phony is bad. So, avoid exaggerations. Try not to seem too anxious. Be polite. Don't smoke. Leave when the producer indicates that the interview is over.

These are some of the things you should not do; conversely, let me say that I think it is necessary for the actor to be friendly and responsive and to treat the whole business as objectively as possible. It seems frightfully personal, but it is best to think of it as just business.

According to one producer, actors fail to present themselves in the best light "when they don't want to be there in the first place. In other words, when an agent or manager has insisted that an actor attend a certain audition even though he or she is wrong for the part. When the actor doesn't want to be there, it comes across to those doing the casting. When an actor wants to audition and truly wants the job, the audition procedure is at its best."

The most common single asset of actors approaching an office, whether they have been in before or not, is preparedness. They can be prepared in many ways.

First, read the play. It seems inconceivable that an actor would come into an office and ask for a job in a play without having made every effort to read or see it. Producers are amazed when they ask actors what part they would like to read for to find that they are totally ignorant of the play or the novel from which the play was adapted. Of course, it is impossible for an actor, in most cases, to read a new play for which he or she may want to audition. But actors can prepare in other ways, and can, for example, be certain that pictures they have submitted to various offices are up to date.

One should not come into an office dressed for a day at the beach. Regardless of the artistic aspects of the theater, it is a business and one that pays rather well when actors are employed.

A prominent Broadway director told me:

> If it were possible via yoga or some similar method of enormous control for the actor to leave his nerves in the waiting room and bring into the interview his own relaxed personality, everyone

would benefit. The artificial office personality is transparent and doesn't allow a real appraisal of the actor's suitability for a part.

I believe that most directors—as they should—know exactly what they are looking for when casting. Some of the qualities they are seeking can be verbalized—some are intuitive and "chemical" and cannot be described. Under these circumstances, I feel that the actor gains nothing in pressing for explanations or indulging in excessive persuasion.

The director is looking for an indication of whether or not the actor, within his own frame of reference, can encompass the essential qualities of the character in the play. This can best be determined if he will know himself and be himself.

A busy agent in New York offered this advice:

To ascertain the attitude or manner assumed by an actor or actress introducing herself or himself to an agent for the first time, there are only a few certain basic necessities to observe, but I mean necessities.

First, a neat, unobtrusive appearance. Choose simple clothes that you can keep in order yourself, colors that blend and do not soil easily, well-groomed hair, and a light street makeup.

If you do not feel a definite confidence in your ability to sell yourself, here's where your talent must come to the fore—assume an air of self-confidence (not arrogance), always being aware that an agent is giving you the opportunity to establish yourself with him. He is a merchant and must have the correct merchandise to sell. He cannot take chances with unknown material, or he sacrifices the confidence of his clients. So try to understand his problem as well as yours. Be as brief as possible in your first interview.

When an agent asks you about yourself, don't fumble for your portfolio and reach for the inevitable photograph and résumé. He'll ask for them if and when he wants them. Try to tell him briefly what you have done and why you think you might be of value to him.

If he places you on file and tells you to keep in touch with the office, come in occasionally, repeat your name often so that he attaches it to your appearance in his memory, and leave quickly, unless he asks you to wait. Don't say, "Oh, I bet you've forgotten little me and don't even remember my name." No doubt he has.

The Audition

An audition is a reading of part of a script (if you are an actor) or the performance of dance steps or a song, in other words, the actual competition for the job.

Why does a performer have to audition? Because, at least for now, no one has come up with a better way to cast. Michael Shurtleff, a renowned casting director and teacher, offered valuable insights in his book *Audition: Everything an Actor Needs to Know to Get the Part*. Mr. Shurtleff noted that "Being an actor takes twenty-four hours of each day, and over half of that is spent in trying to get a job rather than in performing it." Preparation for getting the job is what his book is about.

Auditioning for Stage, Television, and Movies

Auditions for plays are usually held on a bare stage in an empty theater, with the director, producer, casting director, choreographer, dramatist, or whoever else is concerned sitting out front, usually in the dark. Probably not all these people will be present for the first reading. When the field of competition is narrowed, those actors still in contention are called back, sometimes several times.

Most often you will be asked to read opposite the stage manager or an assistant or someone not even remotely similar to the character called for in the script. Sometimes (but not often) you will be asked to read "cold" (with no opportunity to look at the script in advance). Don't hesitate to ask—politely but firmly—for a chance to study the scene privately for a few minutes before reading for any part.

These conditions are generally true of readings for television and films as well, except that in all probability, your audition will take place in the office of the casting director, with the participants seated in chairs, rather than standing in the center of a bare stage. In the old days of motion pictures, screen tests were common practice—that is, the person under consideration would actually be filmed playing a scene with other actors (complete with sets, props, and costumes), and the film would be seen by the producer and director in the studio projection room before the part was cast. There are three reasons why this is seldom done anymore: it is too expensive; with the current realistic trend in films, physical features that photograph flawlessly are no longer a requisite; and actors whose abilities are unknown are not usually engaged for important parts in films or television.

When you are called to audition and are not given a script, plan to use interesting or new material. Emily's speeches from *Our Town* and the death scene from *St. Joan* both have been done before. Keep it new, keep it simple, and keep away from Shakespeare—at least for auditioning.

Here are some other hints to consider when you audition:

- Casting directors get bored hearing the same material over and over. One prominent casting director suggests that as a rule of thumb, if you know two other people who are doing the same monologue as you are—don't do it. He also suggests that the performer announce the passage and cite the play being used for the audition. One casting director recently admitted that sometimes he is so busy trying to figure out where the monologue is from that he doesn't pay much attention to how it is being performed.

- Take your time; relax. Don't let nerves get the best of you and force you to speed up the pace. There's nothing as effective as a pause. Listen to the person you are reading with and make eye contact whenever possible.
- When auditioning for a television program, you are not as likely to have to read as often as you do for a play. Some useful information about auditioning for television appeared in *Stand By*, the magazine published by the New York Local of AFTRA. (It's one of the things you get for your dues.)
- When asked about the kind of audition material an actor should choose, a television casting director in New York said: "Anything current. Nothing belonging to a certain period or that requires special makeup and costumes."
- A television director said that "in auditioning for a part, an actor should show some interest and enthusiasm about working. And, if it's not asking too much, he should please be neat and come to appointments on time."
- When asked, "What ultimately wins the part for an actor in your show?" the director answered: "The casting ultimately ends with the actor doing something his own way. From the casting point of view, it's individualism that gets one actor a job over another. Talent, of course, is assumed. 'You're lucky I'm here' is a helpful attitude for the actor who is auditioning. The actor must be able to see himself in the role."

Agnes Nixon, creator, packager, and writer of some of the most successful long-running daytime television series, volunteered this word to the wise for actors auditioning for a show: "They should ask questions if they don't understand. Convey to the people that they're cooperative and interested in doing the job. Sometimes, people are wrong for the part, but they do a very interesting audition. Many times they will be called back for other things, even though they weren't right for the part."

Auditioning for Musicals

If you are auditioning for a musical, know the key you sing in so that you can tell it to the accompanist. Here, too, try to use new or original material. Have two numbers prepared, in case you are lucky enough to be given time for two. One should be a "belt" selection and the other a ballad, both designed to show your versatility and range.

Back Stage, the New York casting newspaper, interviewed the casting directors of Broadway's leading musicals and published their advice. This is a summary of what they had to say:

- If possible, be familiar with the show and which specific role you might be right for. If it's a revival, at least listen to the cast album, if there is one.
- Don't go to an audition for a role that you're not right for. You're not only wasting the casting director's time, but you're leaving him or her with a negative impression of you.
- Choose audition material that's right for you and shows off your talents best.
- Try to avoid material that's too obscure. While there is always a danger in doing material that is overdone, you must also not use material for a musical audition that a pianist will have trouble playing.
- Don't be too friendly and don't talk too much. Everyone at an audition is there to do a job, not make friends. Time is always limited.

You can't expect to be a star overnight. Working as a performer is about building a career. "You work your way up," says director/choreographer Rob Marshall. "It's a natural progression. Look at it as building blocks. All of your experiences are important and they will lead up to something. But, absolutely the most important thing is to keep working and keep trying to be better at your craft."

Auditioning for Commercials

Auditioning for a television commercial (as opposed to a dramatic program) imposes very special requirements. This, too, is almost always done in the office of the network or the advertising agency (usually in New York, Los Angeles, or Chicago), where the agencies have their main offices. But with videotape and VCRs, your audition probably will be taped and either played back instantly or shown later to the client (the sponsor of a commercial) and the producer. In all likelihood, your audition for a commercial will be done for the casting director with no frills or flattering lights.

There are two types of work on television commercials: "on camera" and "off camera." On camera means just what it says. You are in front of the camera, and if your commercial is one of those that actually gets on the air, your picture is seen on the television screen. Off-camera work constitutes only the use of your voice. You narrate the commercial (do a "voice-over") while the picture of stampeding cattle or a dripping sinus is shown on the tube.

Just as important as a photo and résumé for today's actor who hopes to do commercials (and everybody does!) is an audition tape of your voice, on which you read a short series of imagined (or better yet, real) commercials. These should be prepared in consultation with an agent (if you work through one) or with the advice of fellow actors who have already cut their tapes.

A busy voice-over agent had this to say to *Back Stage West* about breaking into voice-overs:

> In the area of voice-over talent development, workshops are very important. Taking classes is one of the only means by which you can get the education necessary for this kind of work. They provide content and context, do's and don'ts practice on real copy, and help prepare you for the kind of demo tape that is a requisite part of this business. There are specifics that need to be communicated through that tape, since it is the major tangible representation of your voice-over talent. Class work is critical throughout an actor's experience. It informs the beginner of the basics and it provides working professionals with a forum in which to practice and develop the skills they use on a daily basis. It's like physical workouts in that a person can go to the gym for the rest of their lives and never be "finished" working out. Similarly, a person's talent is an ever-evolving organism that can always benefit from fresh ideas and continued practice.

You can't get anywhere without a decent voice-over tape. Since they are expensive, it's best to do it right. Use a reliable studio. Also talk to others who have a tape and get referrals.

Auditions for Singers and Dancers

Theatrical stage auditions for singers and dancers are somewhat different, and even more difficult. Each category of performer (i.e., male dancers, male singers, female dancers, female singers) is auditioned separately.

At a typical audition for female dancers that I recently witnessed in New York, three hundred dancers showed up. They gained entrance to the theater, and changed into their dancing clothes if they hadn't worn them to begin with. They were ushered onto the stage in groups of ten and lined up for the "typing out." This means that all dancers whose physical appearance did not suit the requirements of that particular script (too tall, too thin, or what have you) were dismissed immediately, regardless of their dancing abilities.

After the "typing out" was over, fewer than half the dancers were left. The others might have been better dancers, or their appearance might have been ideally suited to another play, but they were immediately out of contention for this particular production.

The remaining dancers were given numbers and shown a combination of dance steps, executed by the assistant choreographer. Each was asked to repeat the combination in turn, and as she left the stage, the choreographer called "wait" or "go" to her. When this phase of the audition ended, about sixty were left. Another combination was demonstrated, and the remaining dancers repeated it. Soon only thirty dancers remained. These were the finalists. They would be called back for the finals on another day.

At the finals, the winnowing down continued and many of the dancers were also asked to sing. Finally, twelve dancers were chosen, five of whom had worked with the choreographer before.

It was the same with the male dancers, male singers, and female singers, except that most of the singers were also asked to dance before they got the jobs.

Here are some things you don't want to do when you go for an audition:

- Don't clear your throat ostentatiously.
- Don't say you have a cold or bronchial pneumonia, or whatever.
- If you sing or dance to the accompaniment of the pianist, work out the tempo and the music in advance, and keep it simple and short. Don't use the verse to songs.
- Don't hand the pianist the score for a Wagner opera and take three or four minutes explaining which sections to play.

If, after your audition, they say "thank you," don't act as if you've been slapped. It doesn't mean they are not considering you. It might mean only that they have more people to see before they make a decision.

Advice

Back Stage, the weekly newspaper for the performing arts, published quotes that had been gathered from producers of summer theaters around the country about what they look for at auditions. Here's a sample of what some producers had to say:

- "I look for a natural stage presence and sincerity more than acting technique. Is the person comfortable on the stage? Does he or she make eye contact with me, acknowledge my presence as 'the audience'? Part of the magic of theater, I think, is the opportunity it affords for the performers and the audience to connect."

- "Come prepared for your audition. Most people I see are very well prepared to interview, but they haven't put nearly enough thought into the audition itself. You see too many people at auditions whose presence, honesty, and believability on the stage are about a negative two, but if you talk to those same people at callbacks, you find they are intelligent and capable individuals."

- "Make your performance short and powerful. Remember, with auditions it is always a long day, both for the actors and the casting people."

- "We are looking for warmth—audiences, actors, even producers. You look for warmth in people and are attracted by it. Warmth establishes a contact between us that is all too rare, unforgettable, and electric."

- "I strongly object to 'shock value' audition pieces, simply because after the fifth or sixth time, the shock value is gone, and there's nothing there. It gets very boring."

- "I like to see a person do something they can do, and not over-reach their grasp, and not put on a big show. All this business of starting with your back to the audience, lowering your head, and 'getting into your character' is just a big show. I look for honesty in a performance. When I see a nineteen-year-old walk out and recite a soliloquy from *Hamlet*, I may learn something about that person's ego, but I don't learn a thing about his ability as an actor. Shakespeare takes years. Acting is not glitter; it's guts. I want to see people laboring honestly at their task."

- "People shouldn't do something vastly out of their age range. A twenty-year-old college student can never be a believable King Lear, no matter how good he is."

- "Whether you do a classical or contemporary audition piece, choose something that displays your vocal range, your stage presence, and your versatility as an actor."

- "Wear appropriate clothes. If you have one lump in the wrong place, forget leotards. Don't dress like a hooker, gypsy, or bag lady, unless you are looking to be cast as one. Do a piece that has something to do with your age and ability. Stop swearing. I have heard all those words, and they are boring. They no longer shock or amuse. They only show immaturity and a lack of taste."

- "Bring copies of your résumé with you, and pay attention to details on the résumé, like phone number and address. You'd be surprised how many résumés I see that lack that basic information."

- "If you want to 'act only' in summer theater, forget it. Most producers want a well-rounded cast who can perform willingly any task assigned."

- "Please introduce yourself and tell me what you are going to do; just the title and character, not the whole plot. Please smile (easy, but everyone forgets). Don't telegraph mistakes or your own personal review or evaluation of your audition. Let me decide for myself. Look like you are glad to be on that stage—or else why should I hire you?"

The prospect of auditions never ends; the competition for roles in all media is so intense that featured players with years of experience may still be required to audition or read. One of the most discouraging aspects of the whole procedure is that you are seldom told that you didn't get the part. The chorus performer, at least, knows that being dismissed after the "finals" means that he or she is no longer being considered. But when a featured performer is told, "Thank you, we'll let you know," even after a third reading, no conclusions can be safely drawn one way or the other, except that notification will be made if he or she has been hired.

When your audition or reading is over, don't loiter backstage waiting for news or ask, "How did I do?" Nobody will tell you anyway, and your anxiety will not help you get the job. If an agent has submitted you for a reading, he or she can often find out where you stand when you can't. One other thing: as soon as the audition or reading is over, try to forget it; concentrate on the next. There's nothing more discouraging or useless than sitting around wondering why you didn't get the part. It is important to understand that there are many factors that influence casting over which you have absolutely no control. Don't torture yourself over it; just continue to do your best. Remember that each script has peculiar demands; each producer and director has idiosyncrasies and preferences.

Auditioning is a tough business and full of rejection, but don't allow the discouragement to trap you into trying to duplicate the personality of some established star. In the final analysis, your individuality is the only thing you have to sell; if you can retain that, you'll be better able to fulfill yourself and your assignment when opportunity does come.

Some Final Hints

Recently, I interviewed more than forty people in the industry—agents, casting directors, producers, and directors, people who are familiar with the hiring process—for an article for *AFTRA Magazine*. Here's what some of them had to say:

- Sending unsolicited tapes to anybody is a waste of money. If someone, after seeing your picture and résumé and meeting you, wants to see a tape, he or she will say so. Just be sure that person knows you have one and are willing to part with it.
- Casting directors will often ask an actor to do a scene and sometimes will make a tape of the audition to show the director and producer. Even if you're not often asked for a tape, it's a good idea to have one. Be sure it's of good quality. Going into an empty room and videotaping yourself, or simply sitting on a bench and having someone feed you lines is no good. And if the lighting on the tape is bad, that doesn't help you either. A good tape should run about seven minutes. It should consist of the best scenes from whatever professional work you've done. It's not easy or inexpensive to get a decent tape.
- Most casting directors and agents advise actors not to sit back and wait for the agent to make the big break for them. People should try to get into a showcase and then invite directors, casting directors, and producers. Send out response cards for people to check when someone from their office can come to see you. Obvi-

ously, when you're cast in a television show, or anything else worth watching, you get the word out in similar ways: notify everybody you can think of and try to get them to see it.

So far so good, so let's recap: You've got a great headshot, a brief résumé that tells where you've been, and an impressive seven-minute tape. Now what?

You've got an audition or interview. How do you dress? The consensus is that if the script doesn't call for it, don't show up in a torn T-shirt or jeans.

"Be prepared" is more than the Boy Scout motto; it's the unanimous advice of everybody in the business. If you're going for a specific role, find out as much about it and the project as possible. Most important is being professional, being prepared. If you're doing a monologue, do something that's right for you. Don't do Shakespeare unless you're interviewing for a Shakespeare festival. A mistake many actors make is picking a scene that's not right for them, something that's too much of a stretch in terms of character or age.

The single quality that most favorably impresses everybody when they meet an actor is confidence. You want to give the impression that you are the best person for the job; you don't want in any way to convey desperation. That just turns people off.

3

WHERE THE JOBS ARE— AND HOW MUCH THEY PAY

MOST ACTORS WILL work anywhere—anywhere there is a stage, a camera, or an audience—whether they are paid or not. But it is important to determine early on if acting is going to be a vocation (the work in which a person is regularly employed) or an avocation (a subordinate occupation pursued in addition to one's vocation, especially for enjoyment; a hobby). We are going to address acting as a vocation, pursuing it as a career to earn a living in—on stage, screen, or television.

Professional work on the stage includes: Broadway; out-of-town or road companies of Broadway shows; touring companies of shows that may or may not have originated on Broadway and may or may not ever get to Broadway; regional theaters; dinner theaters; off-Broadway, off-off Broadway, and similar small theaters in Los Angeles, Chicago, and San Francisco, many of which consist of workshop and nonprofessional productions; summer stock; children's theater; and many university theater groups.

Everyone who works professionally in these areas (exclusive of workshop productions) is a member of Actors' Equity Association, the union administering jurisdiction over the live legitimate theater.

Broadway

The minimum wage on Broadway, effective June 2004, was $1,381 per week, and it's projected to be more than $1,500 in 2008. Most chorus members (singers and dancers in musical shows) work for minimum or close to it. Principal actors (those playing larger speaking parts) often negotiate higher salaries for themselves.

Stars of Broadway productions may earn much more than minimum per week, plus a percentage of the gross receipts. Rehearsal and performance salaries are the same. Dramatic productions may rehearse up to eight weeks, and musicals may rehearse for nine weeks for principals and ten weeks for chorus.

There are also numerous fringe benefits negotiated by the union, including health insurance coverage, employer contributions to a pension plan, a 401(k) retirement plan, and paid vacations.

Regional Theater

The growth of theater away from such traditional areas as Broadway began in the 1960s, and by 1966 it had proliferated to the point that a new department and separate contract had to be created by Actors' Equity Association to deal specifically with this new phenomenon. There are professional resident theaters in half the states of the union, including such well-known and long-established theaters as the Cleveland Playhouse; Alley Theater in Houston, Texas; the Goodman Theater in Chicago; Center Stage in Baltimore; Mark Taper Forum in Los Angeles; Actors' Theater of Louisville in Kentucky; the Guthrie Theater in Minneapolis; Yale University School of Drama; McCarter Theater Company at Princeton University; American Conservatory Theater in San Francisco; and the Arena Stage in Washington, D.C.

Sometimes, productions that have their origins in resident theaters meet with such critical acclaim that they may be moved to Broadway.

Minimum salaries for regional theaters (under Equity's League of Resident Theaters, or LORT, contract) are based on seating capacity and potential gross of the theater; but they range from around $500 per week to more than $700.

Dinner Theater

Dinner theaters, though their numbers have declined considerably in recent years, remain a good source of employment for actors. There are professional dinner theaters in about half the states in the union. Dinner theaters may accommodate up to a thousand patrons, ranging downward in size to fewer than 150 seats. Equity's Dinner Theater Agreement covers theaters presenting consecutive productions where dinners are served either in the same room in which the performance is given or in an adjacent room. Dinner theater agreements are negotiated separately for each dinner theater in each regional area and have differing salary scales. Each production must play no fewer than three weeks and the theater must operate on a year-round basis. The advertised admission price must include both the meal and the performance; however, 25 percent of the performances in any given week may be on a performance-only basis. There are many non-union dinner theaters around the country that also are a good source of employment.

Off-Broadway

The off-Broadway theater took hold in the early 1950s as an off-shoot of the more "commercial" Broadway theater. It developed primarily in converted Greenwich Village lofts and basements. Once it was considered the ideal way to break into the so-called "big time" and gain notice without too much experience, because few of the more experienced actors would work for the salaries offered. As late as 1961, rehearsals for off-Broadway shows paid only $20 a week, and salaries after opening began at $45. Here, too, salaries are now based on size and the potential box office gross of the theater. The minimum ranges from less than $500 per week in the smallest theaters (from 100 to 199 seats) to more than $800 per week in the largest theaters (351 to 499 seats) for both rehearsal and performance. Off-Broadway productions now get as much attention from drama critics in the large metropolitan newspapers as do the plays uptown on Broadway. Some of the most exciting work in the New York theater has been done off-Broadway.

The phenomenal very rapid development of off-Broadway theater represented, in Tennessee Williams's words, "the greatest new thing that has happened to the American theater, because really experimental things can be done at such low cost. The thing that prohibits experiment on Broadway," Mr. Williams said, "is the tremendously enormous cost of experiment." Since he first expressed that view, however, the cost of mounting even an off-Broadway production has increased. Nonetheless, this cost is still considerably less than the "cost of experiment" on Broadway.

To qualify as an off-Broadway "house" in terms of computing salaries, a theater is usually located outside the immediate Broadway theater area. Also, it may not seat more than 499 persons; 199 seats are usual. While most actors working off-Broadway settle for close to the minimum salary, here, as on Broadway, actors may negotiate higher salaries.

There are other considerations, too, and as is the case with most union contracts, the off-Broadway agreement is rather complex. When one becomes a member of a union, it is advisable to check with it the details of the particular contract under which the actor works. Many of the problems between actors and producers stem from a failure by the members to contact their unions when they begin working. In addition, many actors do not bother to learn the details of their contracts before signing them.

Off-Off Broadway

As production costs increased and off-Broadway gained more recognition, it was inevitable that it, too, would "go commercial." At this time, off-off Broadway theater appeared, along with the Equity Showcase Code, to protect the professional actors appearing in these productions. A showcase, by Equity's definition, is a nonprofit production participated in by Equity members for the purpose of presenting scenes and/or a play for the benefit of the participating actors in limited semipublic performance. No obligatory admission fee in any form is paid. One show that began as a showcase and went on to far greater glory was *A Chorus Line*.

But off-off Broadway is mainly for the nonprofessional. It is here, in the lofts and basements, that experimentation and learning may still flourish without risk of financial disaster.

Stock

Stock used to be the traditional "meat and potatoes" of the acting profession. It was the fertile soil from which many outstanding talents have sprung and grown. More than fifty years ago, there were hundreds of stock companies flourishing throughout the country, and the resident actor, impelled by necessity and constant exposure, often worked fifty weeks a year.

Employment in summer stock is declining annually. (A stock company is one that rehearses a particular show and performs it in the evenings, while rehearsing the subsequent production during the day.)

Summer stock employment peaked in 1964. Reasons for the current decline include rising costs, which are forcing small-capacity theaters out of existence. Also, large musical theaters have found it more profitable to present variety shows headlining television and recording stars.

Another kind of stock company is the large outdoor musical theater. These companies seat thousands of people, employ casts of up to fifty performers, and mount productions every bit as lavish as their Broadway counterparts.

In nonresident dramatic stock companies, the so-called straw hat circuit that usually hires stars to tour in their productions, the minimum weekly salary for an actor goes from around $600 to about $800 weekly.

In stock, actors pay for their own food and lodging, but unless they are making well over the minimum salary, the producer must find them reasonable accommodations and places to eat. There are also numerous fringe benefits, such as health insurance coverage, transportation of baggage, and cleaning of personal clothes worn in productions. Transportation from city to city, if one is working in stock on the road or filming "on location," is paid by the producer.

Performing in an outdoor drama is another way to spend an exciting summer. Most companies perform historical pageants and employ large casts. These companies provide an opportunity to work with Hollywood stunt people and are a combination of summer camp and Western movies. Union theaters pay a minimum salary in excess of $600 weekly.

There are also opportunities for young singers and dancers in amusement and theme parks like Disneyland. Here, too, large casts are required. The work schedule is grueling, but the pay is decent and the experience is excellent. Cruise ships provide another venue for singers and dancers who like to travel.

Dramatics magazine, published monthly except June, July, and August by the Educational Theatre Association (a national nonprofit arts service organization dedicated to the advancement of educational theater), annually publishes a comprehensive summer theater directory that includes a state-by-state list of summer theater training programs, university-based study programs, university summer theaters, conservatories and arts schools, professional summer theaters, specialized workshops, summer camps, outdoor drama companies, and amusement and theme parks. The directory includes programs offered, admission requirements, and name of the person to contact for information. Included, too, are Canadian and international training grounds.

Subscription information for *Dramatics* may be obtained by writing to the Educational Theatre Association, 2343 Auburn Avenue, Cincinnati, Ohio 45219.

Children's Theater

Children's theater, more formally known as Theater for Young Audiences (TYA), provides acting opportunities for both amateur and professional performers. Actors' Equity claimed jurisdiction over this area in 1969 and lists more than sixty-five professional companies throughout the country. However, many more are non-union or community-based and should be investigated as possible sources of employment. In many cases, working with a children's theater group is seasonal (Christmas and spring vacation times or summer) or weekend work, and can be pursued while also working at a paying job. Salaries for Equity actors are less than $400 per week, or in a smaller company with a limited number of performances, paid on a per performance basis. Many actors have received their early training in a Theater for Young Audiences company.

Business Theater

Many stars work in industrial or business theater shows and a few may also be identified with a certain product through television commercials. Industrial shows are those productions (sometimes performed only once) that are paid for by a company and presented to an invited, nonpaying audience. Often the audience consists of the company's employees. Automobile manufacturers may use an industrial show to demonstrate new cars to sales organizations.

In years past, as industry discovered that theatrical techniques were useful in communicating with audiences, these presentations grew in lavishness, and entire production companies were completely devoted to creating and producing industrial shows and films. But today, industrial shows have become more modest in an effort to economize.

Even for the chorus performer or the principal with only two lines, industrial shows are considered choice employment.

There are also numerous fringe benefits associated with union industrial shows, including accident and health insurance, contributions to the pension and health funds, overtime payment, and so forth.

Film for Theater and Television

Motion pictures, which for our purposes shall be defined as anything performed on film (even if shown on television), come under the jurisdiction of the Screen Actors Guild. In addition, some shows done on tape for television viewing are produced under SAG contracts, while some taped shows are produced under the jurisdiction of the American Federation of Television and Radio Artists.

As with the stage, there are different agreements covering various kinds of films. Before television and industrial shows came on the scene, a picture was a picture, and obviously it would be seen by an audience that bought tickets to a neighborhood theater. That situation changed years ago. While there are still pictures filmed for theatrical release, there are also separate conditions for films made for television commercials. There is, too, a separate agreement for background performers and a complex formula for extra payment for recent films that are also shown on television. And, as a result of a strike by members of AFTRA and SAG, there are special payments for films shown at home on new electronic equipment.

Most salaries in feature films (those made originally for theater viewing) are based on daily or weekly rates. The minimum rate for day players is $695 as of July 1, 2004, for an actor who speaks lines. The minimum weekly rate is $2,411 as of July 1, 2004. Most featured players are paid more. Some actors, including stars, are paid by the picture.

Unlike feature films, television films have a special interim pay scale for three days' work, since many half-hour television shows complete most of their shooting in a three-day time span, and there are refinements of these contracts to encompass the filming of multiple episodes of a television series, provisions for overtime, "residual rights," and so forth.

In recent years, residual rights have assumed enormous economic importance to the actor, particularly in the field of filmed television commercials or series. Residual payments may be defined as additional payment to the actor for re-showing on television a play or commercial (on tape or film) in which the actor appeared; the amount of the payment is related to the number of times the program or "spot" (a short commercial shown between programs) is used and the number of cities in which it is shown.

Most actors—even some well-known personalities—do commercials for "scale" (minimum salary), because the real money is made on residuals if the commercial is widely shown. AFTRA and SAG jointly negotiate with employers the scales and conditions for television commercials. Both AFTRA and SAG have special departments that administer the calculation, collection, and payment to members of residual rights.

At this writing, the minimum scale for a principal actor on camera (one who is seen and heard) is $535.70 a day, or per commercial, if more than one spot is filmed on the same day. An "off camera" principal gets $402.25. The system of residual payments for reruns is very complicated, and we will not attempt to break it down in these pages, but as an example, a network program on a camera spot with a thirteen-use guarantee within thirteen weeks will pay the actor about $1,728.55.

I know of actors who went to stock theaters for a summer and returned to find that they had several thousand dollars when they came home, all of which they had earned in residuals while they were gone.

In addition to these payments, the talent unions have established health and retirement funds, to which employers make contributions on behalf of members ranging up to 14.3 percent of their total compensation.

All the wage scales negotiated by the unions are minimum requirements. The actor can be paid as much as he or she can get, but the great majority of performers must be content to work for "scale" (minimum).

There are also contract provisions for residual payments for television films and recent regular feature movies, and many actors who appeared in television serials that are being rerun collect money for those, too.

The current minimum salaries for industrial programs under AFTRA's jurisdiction are:

Category I day performer: $440.00
Category II day performer: $547.00
Category I weekly performer: $1,544.50
Category II weekly performer: $1,912.50

Category I programs are designed to train, inform, promote a product, or perform a public relations function and may be exhibited in classrooms, museums, libraries, or other places where no admission is charged. Included are closed-circuit television transmissions (such as direct broadcasts by satellites) and teleconferences. Included also are sales programs that are designed to promote products or services of the sponsor but that will be shown on a restricted basis only. Category II programs are intended for unrestricted exhibition to the general public.

This brings us to the category of background work in films. If a movie company has worked "on location" (away from the studio) in or near your home, chances are that someone you know has been an extra or background player in the film. Under certain circumstances, it is not necessary to join a union to work as an extra in pictures, particularly if the extras are local residents of a location community and work only once. But many people earn their livelihoods as background players and may earn almost $130 a day when they work, plus such AFTRA and SAG fringe benefits as employer contributions toward retirement and health insurance. There are several categories of background performers, depending on the extent of the duties involved, and the wage scales are adjusted upward accordingly. A background performer in a commercial may receive almost $300 a day, but he or she does not receive residuals.

Television

There is a standard minimum rate for network broadcasting and a wide variance in local rates, depending on where the stations are located.

As with theater and films, most experienced principal actors earn more than the scale salaries for one-shot shows. Those appearing regularly on the few soap operas still left, however, usually work for scale or close to it, in exchange for guarantees of continuous employment for anywhere from thirteen to fifty-two weeks. Taped shows that are shown again offer residual payments to the actors.

AFTRA and SAG have negotiated jointly in the field of prime-time television, so that the rates and repayment structure for prime-time programs are identical for each union, and in some cases, they are higher than for other network shows.

AFTRA has separate contracts covering local and network radio broadcasts, local and network television broadcasts, taped television, sound recordings, transcriptions, and commercials under these separate and individual circumstances. There are numerous subclassifications, fringe benefits, and working conditions that have not been mentioned, including special (and lower) scales for background performers. Then there are other rules and wage levels applying only to announcers, news broadcasters, singers, and sportscasters, for example.

In the field of television, too, the oft-repeated commercial yields high returns. How high? In some cases, in excess of $1,500 for one use in thirteen cities. Imagine the returns from a commercial repeated over and over again in a nationwide advertising campaign!

Whether commercials are performed on film, are done live, or taped on television, they are something quite separate and apart from conventional acting. Many good actors find it virtually impossible to adapt to the "hard sell" technique of looking directly at the camera's lens and "pitching" a product. The actor's job essentially is to relate to other people, and sometimes the only thing available in a commercial is a cake of soap. Conversely, many relaxed and attractive performers, who have no difficulty whatsoever convincing a camera that the thing they would most like to do in the whole world is unclog a sink with a certain product, are not at their best when they are put on stage with other people. Few actors today can afford the luxury of being able to specialize. To survive, they must do everything.

4

STATE OF THE UNIONS

PROFESSIONAL ACTORS BELONG to one or more of three major performing arts unions in the United States:

- Actors' Equity Association (commonly called AEA or Equity) has jurisdiction over the stage.
- The Screen Actors Guild (SAG) covers all film regardless of where it is shown, and it shares with AFTRA jurisdiction over taped programs, commercials (most of which are shot under SAG contracts), and industrial/nonbroadcast presentations.
- The American Federation of Television and Radio Artists (AFTRA) is the union exercising jurisdiction over live television, variety and talk shows, news broadcasts, soap operas, weather reporting, reality and game shows, radio, and sound recordings; in addition, it shares with the Screen Actors Guild (SAG) jurisdiction in the fields of taped prime-

time television programs, taped commercials, and
industrial/nonbroadcast presentations.

Along with other performers' unions, these three organizations
comprise the Associated Actors and Artistes of America (the Four
A's), which is chartered by the AFL-CIO. The Four A's, in turn, has
issued charters to its components so each union administers the
jurisdiction that has been awarded to it. While each union is autonomous in respect to its individual jurisdiction, it is, theoretically at
least, ultimately responsible to its parent body, the Four A's. In reality, this responsibility means very little, for individual unions exer-
cise their separate jurisdictions with practically no help or guidance
from the parent body.

Why Were the Unions Formed?

Equity, the oldest of the three big actors' unions, was formed by
112 actors on May 26, 1913, in New York City. At that time, and
for many years after, motion pictures were considered by the old-
time stage actors to be a temporary and inartistic phenomenon not
worth organizing. Television, of course, did not exist. Since the
legitimate theater was the core of the actor's life, naturally it was
first to organize, and the conditions that led to Equity's establishment were similar to those that actors in films and television either
feared or suffered later on, and which eventually led to the forma-
tion of SAG and AFTRA.

Since the late 1800s, employers in the theater had been
encroaching upon the rights of actors to such an extent that
exploitation had become a permanent condition of employment,
and the plight of the actor was becoming increasingly onerous and

difficult. There was no standard contract, no minimum wage, no fixed conditions, and no predictable number of rehearsals. Examination of an actual (and typical) contract dated May 1913 between a well-known actress and a producer yields the following information: For $20 a week, the actress played in any theater the producer designated; she furnished all gloves, shoes, tights, stockings, lace, feathers, and any modern costume that she owned; she rehearsed for thirteen weeks without any salary whatsoever, and worked seven days a week, giving as many performances as the manager required; she received no salary if the company could not obtain suitable bookings; if the star was unable to perform, the company also went without salary.

In those days, it was common practice to fire actors on opening night (perhaps after four months' rehearsal at no salary); to abscond with the box office receipts; and to leave a cast not only without salary after having worked the week, but stranded anywhere in the country without fare home to New York. In short, the producer set the requirements, and few actors were able to stand against them.

Actors' Equity Association

There had been occasional but unsuccessful attempts by individual actors and actor-managers to combat these impositions. One of these was the organization of the Actors' Society of America about 1896, but that association never became sufficiently strong to establish itself as a protector of the actors. By the winter of 1912, it had become so feeble that a meeting was called to decide whether it was worth continuing, or whether a new association, dedicated solely to the economic problems of the actor, would better serve the purpose. At that first meeting, a "Plan and Scope Committee" was formed to work out the arrangements for a new association. By May

1913, the constitution and bylaws for Actors' Equity Association had been drafted.

But it was not that simple. Powerful theater owners and producers—some of them well-known actors themselves—bitterly fought the fledgling union. George M. Cohan would commit $100,000 of his personal fortune to try to destroy it. For six years, Equity tried to negotiate a contract that all managers would recognize. The producers would not negotiate—would not recognize Equity as the actors' bargaining agent. Equity applied to the American Federation of Labor for affiliation, but it couldn't be accepted because a charter was already outstanding to an organization called the White Rats, composed mainly of vaudeville performers. Hurried negotiations among labor representatives resulted in the White Rats relinquishing their charter, after which the Associated Actors and Artistes of America (The Four A's) was immediately formed in 1919 and chartered by the AFL. The Four A's, in turn, recognized Equity as the union representing actors in theater, and the other group (consisting of former White Rats) as the union representing vaudeville performers. Thus armed with AFL affiliation, Equity went on strike to be recognized.

The strike began on August 7, 1919, and lasted thirty days, until September 6. It spread to eight cities, closed thirty-seven plays, prevented the opening of sixteen others, and cost everybody concerned several millions of dollars. Supported by the International Alliance of Theatrical Stage Employees and the American Federation of Musicians, Equity found in September that its membership had increased from twenty-seven hundred to about fourteen thousand, and its treasury, which had held $13,500 when the strike began, had increased to $120,000, despite the expenditure of more than $5,000 a day. When it was over, the managers had signed a contract for five years that included practically all of Equity's demands.

In thirty days, Equity had been transformed from a nonproductive association of discontented actors into a labor union of recognized authority and influence. But that was not the end of strife. There were to be other battles later, on this and other fields; but the main skirmish had been won. The trend toward union organization by America's actors was clearly underway.

Screen Actors Guild (SAG)

The Screen Actors Guild was formed in 1933. At that time, actors were lucky to be paid $15 for a long day's work or $66 for a six-day week. Unregulated hours and working conditions were even worse than the pay. In March of 1933, producers decreed a 50 percent pay cut for all actors under studio contracts. With no organization or collective bargaining power, the actors took the cut.

As a result of that action by producers, a small group of Hollywood actors got together to talk about forming a self-governed guild of motion picture actors to give performers a stronger voice. Articles of Incorporation were filed in Sacramento in June 1933. A four-year struggle for union recognition and a contract with producers followed.

In 1937, the early members of the Screen Actors Guild voted to strike, if necessary, to achieve union recognition. With over 95 percent of the major stars of that time ready to walk off the job, the producers backed down, and on May 9, 1937, SAG signed its first contract governing wages and working conditions for actors in feature films.

Since then, through collective bargaining with producers, SAG has created a new and better working environment for performers by establishing regular working hours, meal periods, a five-day week, and pay for working overtime, Sunday, and holidays. Successive contracts have brought increased wages for all performers, pension and health plans paid by the producer, residual payments for reuse of motion pictures and television programs, regulation of talent agents and their commissions, and safety standards on the set.

Former U.S. President Ronald Reagan served as an officer of the Guild from 1941 to 1960, including six terms as president.

American Federation of Television and Radio Artists (AFTRA)

In the mid-1930s, America was in economic depression, but radio was booming. In 1936, radio was the fourth-largest industry in America. In 1937, it collected more than $140 million in advertising revenue. True, stars were earning large weekly salaries. However, for those who were not stars, conditions were quite different. Performers might be paid anything from $5 to $50 per performance, including hours or days of rehearsal. In addition, they might be expected to play multiple characters on one show for the single fee, and if a pilot show didn't make it onto the air, they wouldn't be paid at all. And, if they didn't like the terms, hundreds of others were eager to take their places.

Performers already had discovered the benefits of unionism. The American Federation of Musicians and Actors' Equity were already on the scene and film actors were organizing into the Screen Actors Guild when, in 1935, a group of twenty-one Los Angeles radio performers got together to see what they could do. But the "21 Club," as they called it, never got off the ground. Six months into its existence, several radio stations got wind of the enterprise and threatened—on station letterhead—to blacklist any performer involved. The club dissolved.

The second attempt at organization was more successful. Some radio actors learned that the Congress of Industrial Organizations (CIO) was planning to organize radio performers as part of the Telegraphers Union. The radio performers then held a hasty meeting in Hollywood and the result was the Radio Artists Guild (RAG).

At the same time, Actors' Equity, which had jurisdiction over radio performers, was also exploring some sort of organization in New York. The two groups got together in New York on July 17, 1937, with representatives of the Screen Actors Guild, Equity, and the newly formed (1936) American Guild of Musical Artists (which has jurisdiction over opera, ballet, and concert performers) to form a new national union, the American Federation of Radio Artists (AFRA). As with the other unions, recognition of the union by employers did not come easily. It was not until July 12, 1938, that AFRA signed the first collectively bargained agreement on a national scale with NBC and CBS. This Basic Network Sustaining Agreement established a wage increase of 125 percent and a union shop agreement for radio talent.

In the mid and late 1940s, television began to capture the public's imagination and dollars. Radio shows and personalities began the move over to television. But television performers were not organized. AFRA and SAG were fighting for jurisdiction. So on April 16, 1950, the Associated Actors and Artistes of America created a new organization, Television Authority (TVA), with jurisdiction over television actors. TVA negotiated the first network television contract in December 1950. On September 17, 1952, TVA and AFRA merged to create a new union with a "T": AFTRA, the American Federation of Television and Radio Artists.

AFTRA and SAG have been talking about merging for decades. In 1974, the two unions negotiated jointly for the first time for a contract covering prime-time dramatic programming. They continue to negotiate several contracts together, maintain joint offices in several cities around the country, and still talk about merger. The most recent failed merger attempt was in 2003.

Will Joining a Union Get You a Job?

Many newcomers feel that getting a union card is the most important step toward furthering a career. They assume that once they have joined Equity, SAG, or AFTRA, they will automatically find employment, or at least their chances will be better than they were before membership. This isn't necessarily true: in fact, the opposite sometimes applies. Unions are absolutely essential to the actor, but membership in an actors' union is no guarantee of getting a job, and joining a union prematurely might actually impede your career. Here's why:

Except in a few special circumstances, most performer unions require (insofar as the law allows) their members to work with other union members; they are usually, except in special circumstances, discouraged from acting with nonprofessional groups. These rules are perfectly proper and are designed to protect professional actors from exploitation. But a novice in the field usually finds it difficult to keep busy in professional companies. Often amateur, community, and school groups offer the newcomer valuable experience through work that the newcomer may not be free to take if he or she is a union member. It may be the wrong move to join a union too early and eliminate some opportunities for gaining valuable experience.

Amy Dolan, who began as a child performer and has worked on stage and in television commercials, is Equity's National Education and Outreach Coordinator. She advises against joining the union too soon. She says that a performer shouldn't consider the union until he or she has decided that acting is going to be a career, not a hobby, and that he or she is ready to compete in the business. On the other hand, she cautions, it is also possible to wait too long to join.

What Do the Unions Do?

The unions do not get you jobs. They do protect you in your relations with employers. They negotiate and police enforceable contracts, which guarantee specific minimum salaries and provisions for extra payment for extra work. They obtain and enforce certain working conditions that the members want, and they guarantee that salaries will be paid. In addition, SAG, AFTRA, and Equity all have pension and health plans, financed by employer contributions. These were hard fought for, long in coming, and are of great significance. The purpose of these plans is to provide health insurance benefits to covered members and to offer them some measure of financial security, based on a system of tenure, seniority, earnings, and continuity of employment.

AFTRA offers several scholarships to eligible members or their children. These include some that were established in the memory of past union leaders and are available for any course of study. There is also one provided specifically for the study of any branch of music, and one offering aid for vocal coaching. These are administered through the AFTRA Heller Memorial Foundation, named in honor of George Heller, one of AFTRA's founders. There are a number of college scholarships for eligible AFTRA members or their children for general study, study of the performing arts, and labor relations. The SAG Foundation administers the John L. Dales Scholarship Fund, created in honor of a former executive.

The unions offer group medical insurance, legal counseling, and some casting information. They publish magazines and newsletters that are mailed periodically to members and offer assistance on problems such as unemployment insurance and relations with agents. These organizations also attempt to influence legislation that will assist the performing arts and artists on civic, state, and national levels. This is done through membership in the Department for Professional Employees of the AFL-CIO. In addition, members offer suggestions for new contracts and serve on negotiating committees, thereby having an actual hand in establishing their own wages and working conditions.

Crucial to the unions' ability to enforce their contracts and protect actors is the actors' understanding of their obligations and duties, not only as professional performers, but as union members. Unhappily, too few actors understand this, and they are often reminded, painfully and suddenly, that their union membership is a two-way street: they derive enormous benefits and protection, but they must also comply with all terms of the contracts they have signed. Unions protect employers, too, and woe to the actor who fails to fulfill her or his contractual obligations. Such conduct is considered unforgivable in every branch of show business, and the governing boards of the unions, customarily lenient and generous with their fellow performers, do not tolerate it.

The range of services provided by actors' unions is wide—from the disbursement of residual payment checks by AFTRA and SAG to the listing of available apartments in New York on the bulletin board of Actors' Equity. Each union has a website, booklets, pamphlets, and other information available to new and old members, explaining its rules, services, and jurisdiction, and telling whom to see for other specific information. The first thing you should do when you join a union is to get all this information and read it.

Whenever an actor gets into trouble with respect to a job or the union, it is almost always caused by ignorance of the rules.

The unions are anxious to be consulted by members with questions, no matter how trivial or irrelevant their questions may seem. But often the union does not find out about a problem in time to prevent it. These organizations can be effective only if their members cooperate. Too often newcomers who do not know the historic values and traditions of the acting profession consider themselves too "artistic" to be concerned with mundane things like rules—or else they are too lazy, too selfish, or so anxious to work in a competitive profession that they are willing to sacrifice the mutual gains won by others through many years of work.

How Are the Unions Governed?

While there are numerous differences between the government and administration of the unions, the foundations of their governments are essentially the same. Each has an elected board of directors or council, which is always composed of members who serve without compensation. In this respect, the actors' unions are different from other labor organizations in that the presidents, officers, and board members of Equity, SAG, and AFTRA receive no pay.

These governing boards meet regularly to determine matters of policy. The policies are executed and administered by a paid staff of executives.

When and How Do You Join?

Although most young performers are extremely anxious to join the actors' unions, the unions themselves do not recruit new members with any visible enthusiasm. They have enough problems trying to find jobs for their already large proportion of unemployed. Before joining a union, one is supposed to be an actor of serious purpose with prospects of employment in the field.

Specifically, then, having already learned something about jurisdiction, services, and common functions of the unions, let us explore on an individual basis their dues structures, membership requirements, and other relevant data.

Actors' Equity

If a producer offers an actor an Equity contract in any branch of the union's jurisdiction, the actor then joins Equity. Performers who have been members of another Four A's union (AFTRA or SAG, for instance), for one year or longer and have performed under that union's jurisdiction any work that is comparable to that of a principal, or specifically defined extra work, are also eligible to join Equity.

Another alternative is to join through the Equity Membership Candidate Program at one of the many participating Equity theaters. The program allows nonprofessional actors to credit their work toward Equity membership. After fifty weeks at accredited theaters, the registered membership candidate may join the union.

Membership candidates are credited every week they rehearse, perform, or understudy with an Equity company. The fifty weeks need not be consecutive nor worked at the same theater, provided that the work occurs at an Equity theater where the program is in effect.

After securing a nonprofessional position at a participating Equity theater, the candidate registers as a membership candidate by completing an Equity nonprofessional affidavit provided by the theater and sends the affidavit plus a $100 registration fee payable to Equity. This one-time fee is credited against the initiation fee that becomes due upon joining the union.

After accumulating fifty workweeks as a membership candidate, eligibility to join Equity lasts for a five-year period, but the candidate may no longer work at an Equity theater unless he or she signs an Equity contract and joins the union. Since the membership candidate is not yet a member of Equity but is working toward membership, the protections and privileges enjoyed by members cannot be extended to the membership candidate. Members of other entertainment industry unions must make special application to Equity to participate in this program.

Equity's initiation fee is $1,100. Basic dues are $118 per year. Additionally, there are also working dues; these are 2.25 percent of gross earnings from employment under Equity's jurisdiction, up to a maximum amount based on earnings of $300,000 or less.

Like SAG, Equity is governed by a central council; the union has regional offices, but no locals, and while the branch offices are, in practice, somewhat autonomous in their executive administration, they are subject to policies set forth by the council. Equity's headquarters are at 165 West Forty-Sixth Street, New York, New York 10036. Regional offices are located in the following cities: 125 South Clark Street, Chicago, Illinois 60603; 5757 Wilshire Boulevard, Los Angeles, California 90036; 350 Sansome Street, San Francisco, California 94104; and 10319 Orangewood Boulevard, Orlando, Florida 32821. Equity also has liaisons in cities around the country including Atlanta, Boston, Cleveland, Dallas/Fort Worth, Denver, Detroit, Houston, Kansas City, Las Vegas, Miami, Minneapolis, Nashville, Philadelphia, Phoenix, Pittsburgh, St. Louis, San Diego, Seattle, and Washington/Baltimore.

Since Equity was created in 1913, actors have moved a long stride forward. None of the unions can get actors jobs, nor can they always keep jobs for them. Collectively and individually, each union's greatest problem is the high degree of unemployment among its members. The profession is still a nightmare of pitfalls and insecurities, but whatever protection and stability our actors have achieved, they have done so largely through their unions.

Screen Actors Guild (SAG)

A performer is eligible to join the Screen Actors Guild after meeting the following criteria: He or she has worked one day as a principal performer on a SAG project produced by a signatory company. The performer should have been engaged on a daily, three-day, or weekly contract and paid appropriate wages; or worked a minimum of three days, consecutive or nonconsecutive, as a background performer on any production produced by a signatory company. The three days of work as a background performer do not have to be on the same production, but the performer must have been given a voucher and paid the appropriate background wage. A performer who is a member of AFTRA, Equity, the American Guild of Musical Artists (AGMA), Alliance of Canadian Television and Radio Artists (ACTRA), or American Guild of Variety Artists (AGVA) for at least one year and has worked as a principal performer under the jurisdiction of any of these unions also is eligible for membership in Screen Actors Guild.

To join SAG, a performer must pay an initiation fee of $1,310 plus the first semiannual basic dues of $50. Basic annual dues are $100. In addition, members pay 1.85 percent of all individual earnings under SAG contracts up through $200,000 and 0.5 percent on all individual earnings from $200,000 through $500,000. Dues are calculated on an annual basis and paid in two installments: the first on May 1, and the second on November 1.

Headquartered at 5757 Wilshire Boulevard, Hollywood, California 90036, Screen Actors Guild has branches in many major cities around the country. The New York branch is located at 360 Madison Avenue, New York, New York 10017.

American Federation of Television and Radio Artists (AFTRA)

To join AFTRA, an actor must sign an application and pay an initiation fee (which is currently $1,300) plus dues for the current period. The union consists of a national organization and more than thirty autonomous locals and chapters in major cities across the country.

AFTRA members in New York, as well as other locals, are assessed dues according to a standard schedule. Dues are billed twice a year (May 1 and November 1) and consist of a minimum amount (base dues) plus a small percentage of the member's AFTRA earnings in the previous year. Effective November 2004, the minimum dues were $63.90. Work dues are calculated at 0.743 percent on the first $100,000 in earnings and 0.137 percent on earnings over $100,000. Additional dues are not charged on earnings over $250,000. Members who earn less than $2,000 pay only the base dues; members with earnings $2,000 and up pay dues based on their total earnings. Minimum annual dues are $127.80 and maximum yearly dues are $2,024.80. Dues for members of locals in certain small markets are calculated at a lower rate pursuant to waivers approved by the national board of directors.

Like other unions in the Four A's, AFTRA's major activities have dealt with economic factors: contract negotiations and enforcement and the improvement of wages and working conditions constitute the bulk of AFTRA's functions.

AFTRA's National Headquarters is at 260 Madison Avenue, New York, New York 10016. The New York Local is located at the same address. The Los Angeles Local offices are located at 5757 Wilshire Boulevard, Los Angeles, California 90036. The office of the Chicago Local is at 1 East Erie Street, Suite 650, Chicago, Illinois 60611. Locations of other AFTRA locals are listed in metropolitan telephone books under the name of the organization: American Federation of Television and Radio Artists.

Survival

"Did you study how to use a computer before you became an actress?" I recently asked a talented but little-known actress of my acquaintance when she applied for a temporary job in our office.

"Yes," she said, "my father insisted on it."

"Are you glad?" I asked.

"I sure am. But I hated it at the time. I said, 'Dad, you don't understand. I'm going to be an actor.' He said, 'I understand, but take the computer course first.' It's a good thing he made me do it, or I don't know how I'd eat. I spend nine-tenths of my time working as a secretary and one-tenth acting."

This young person's experience is typical—typical of the lucky ones, that is. Too often, actors and actresses have been so anxious to grab the theater by the throat that they have not taken the time to prepare themselves for survival when the going gets rough.

Survival is an actor's greatest problem, unless he or she has inherited wealth or has wealthy parents so indulgent as to provide support indefinitely.

At a parents' meeting at New York's High School of Performing Arts, a veteran actor once expressed the view that a college education was essential to a theatrical career, "because when you decide to give up the theater, you'll be qualified for another job." He was speaking on the subject of "A Career in Theater." The title of his talk was a misnomer, he said. "Rather, the subject should be 'The Lack of a Career in the Theater and Why You Need a College Education.'"

None of this is very encouraging. It isn't intended to be. But it is enlightening and we may profit from it. Survival in the theater is difficult—success, more difficult still. You must plan for a long period of no acting jobs while you try to establish yourself, and you must have other skills that will enable you to earn a living when you aren't working as an actor. If possible, get a college or business education. Don't be in such a rush to act that you gamble with your entire future.

As a beginning actor in New York or Hollywood, you should start with at least enough money to keep you going for six months without additional income. Not only will you have to support yourself, but you will need extra money to make such necessary business investments as telephone, answering machine, lessons, trade publications, pictures, résumés, and a computer.

Important resources and trade papers for actors are:

• *American Theater Magazine*, published by Theater Communications Group (TCG), 530 Eighth Avenue, New York, New York 10018, contains monthly schedules of productions for regional theaters throughout the country plus other valuable information. TCG membership is $35 per year and includes a subscription to *American Theater Magazine*.

• *ArtSearch*, also published by TCG, is the national employment service bulletin for the arts. It lists openings for administrative, artistic, production, education, and other theater jobs, but no casting information.

- *Back Stage* and *Back Stage West* are the weekly New York and Los Angeles trade papers (or casting bibles of the industry) and contain detailed audition notices—both union and non-union. They are available by subscription or at local newsstands. *Back Stage* is located at 770 Broadway, New York, New York 10003. *Back Stage West* is at 5055 Wilshire Boulevard, Los Angeles, California 90036. For information call (800) 745-8922 or log on to backstage.com.

Back Stage also sponsors the annual Actorfest, trade shows that include an exhibit hall plus seminars and focus sessions. In New York, the exhibit hall traditionally includes more than ninety booths where information is available on all aspects of the industry—from acting schools to photographers. The unions all have booths as well and distribute materials and answer questions throughout the day. Admission to the exhibit hall is free.

Career seminars and/or panel discussions have included such topics as: Does Training Matter?, Working in Independent Films, Adapting to Auditions for Stage and Screen. There are also focus sessions during which participants can interact with agents, casting directors, managers, or other professionals. Topics have included: Marketing Yourself, How to Get an Agent, What's Hot in Commercial Types, Surviving the Audition Process, and more. There are fees for attending the seminars and focus sessions, but they are all led by industry professionals and can be very valuable. For information contact *Back Stage* at backstage.com. A similar event is held in Los Angeles.

- Drama Book Shop, in New York since 1917, is an excellent source for materials on all aspects of the performing arts. There are two levels of books plus space for reading and browsing. It is located at 250 West Fortieth Street, New York, New York 10018; drama bookshop.com.

• Florida Blue Sheet is the premier source for jobs and support in film, television, video, theater, music, writing, voice-overs, print work, and more in Florida. Call: (800) 557-BLUE or visit florida bluesheet.tripod.com.

• Henderson Enterprises, opened in 1983 by Sue Henderson, a working actor, provides information on actor resources and links to other valuable information. It also provides support services and tools and publishes *Casting Directors Guide*. For information go to hendersonenterprises.com.

• Hispanic Organization of Latin Actors (HOLA) is a service organization for Latino actors offering casting referrals, a directory, and more. It's located at 107 Suffolk Street, New York, New York 10001; hellohola.org.

• *Hollywood Reporter* is a trade paper with news of the industry, but no casting information. It's at 5055 Wilshire Boulevard, Los Angeles, California 90036; hollywoodreporter.com.

• Non-Traditional Casting Project maintains a talent bank of actors of color and actors with disabilities. It's at 165 West Forty-Sixth Street, New York, New York 10036; ntcp.org.

• *Performink* is Chicago's theater and film newspaper. It contains audition notices, classified ads, and articles; performink.com.

• *Ross Reports*, a publication of *Back Stage* and *Back Stage West*, lists agents, casting directors, television production, and films in development in both New York and Los Angeles. It is an invaluable guide for television and film work. It's located at 770 Broadway, New York, New York 10013; (646) 654-5730.

• *Show Business Weekly* contains casting and audition notices plus industry information; showbusinessweekly.com.

• *Theatrical Index* is updated weekly and includes information on current and future Broadway and off-Broadway shows, regional companies, and tours. It's at 888 Eighth Avenue, New York, New York 10029; (212) 586-6343.

• *Variety* and *Daily Variety* have news, financial, and other information about the entertainment industry, but no casting information. Go to variety.com.

Expenses

Conard Fowkes is a professional actor who has supported his family in New York for many years. He earns a living as an actor on daytime television dramas, commercials, stage, films, and industrials—in short, in every medium. He belongs to Equity, AFTRA, and SAG and is active in union affairs, thus keeping close tabs on the day-to-day aspects of survival.

Mr. Fowkes reminds us that in addition to the expenses of everyday living, actors have some extra expenses for which they must allow, including coaching and lessons, photos and résumés, hair care, union dues, trade publications, directories, agents' commissions on earnings, and clothing. A writer or painter can perhaps hide behind her or his work, and blue jeans and a sweater may suffice. The actor hides behind nothing—the actor is her or his work, and every actor must have presentable clothes and must keep them cleaned and pressed. You simply don't audition for commercials wearing a dirty dress or wrinkled trousers.

According to Mr. Fowkes, it is not uncommon for young professionals to spend 10 percent of their gross income on acting lessons and another 25 percent on the rent. Add to that Social Security, federal and state taxes, and commissions, and it becomes painfully clear that performers are living in fiscally perilous times.

If it is necessary for you to find a part-time job while looking for work, don't misrepresent yourself; that is, don't mislead your employer into thinking your status is permanent. Several employment agencies specialize in placing part-time or temporary help, and these places may welcome actors, with full knowledge that their main interest lies outside the secretarial field. The classified employment section of the daily newspapers also lists part-time jobs.

Naturally, if you have to find part-time or temporary work, it is preferable to seek hours that will leave you free to pursue your acting career for at least a few hours each day.

To address the problems created by the chronic unemployment and uncertain nature of the entertainment business, the Actors' Work Program was created in 1986 by Actors' Equity Association (although it is now under the aegis of the Actors' Fund of America). It is a project designed to help professionals secure dignified interim employment and/or explore the possibility of developing a second career. The program has greatly expanded since its inception and now includes other members of the entertainment industry along with actors and is funded by most of the entertainment industry unions.

The program helps actors evaluate their skills to find out how they can use their talents in other jobs and conduct an effective job search. Every participant receives individual career counseling and participates in seminars to learn how to prepare résumés and go on interviews. Tuition grants are available for participants to study social work, word processing, teaching English as a Second Language, and other career alternatives.

Career Transition for Dancers (CTFD) is a similar program established specifically to help the dancer, whose career is shorter than that of other performers because of the very physical nature of the work. CTFD offers seminars, workshops, and counseling to assist with career choices. It has offices in New York and Los Angeles.

Rules of the Game

The acting profession has as rigid a set of ethics as any in the world. As you pursue your career, you will sometimes see them violated or sacrificed to expediency, and you will find this hard to accept; not only the worthy are attracted to the acting profession. True professionals live by the rules for the sake of their profession and for themselves.

Here are some do's and don'ts that you as an actor are expected to understand and live by:

- Don't lie about your experience.
- Be honorable in your dealings with agents; don't allow more than one agent to submit you for the same part. (More about this in the next chapter.)
- Be on time for all appointments and rehearsals. Being late for rehearsal is among the worst breaches of theater etiquette. Being late for an interview may cost you the appointment. A casting director probably will keep you waiting; but don't keep the casting director waiting. (This doesn't mean that you should cool your heels in somebody's office for an hour if you are keeping a definite engagement. If you feel, after a reasonable time, that you're being taken advantage of, politely tell the secretary that you cannot wait any longer and make another appointment.)
- When you do get a job, learn your lines as quickly as possible.
- If you accept a job, do your best. Even in a showcase production that pays nothing, you should approach your work as if your entire career depended on it. Maybe it does.

- Don't criticize the other actors with whom you're working or with whom you are in competition. If you're up for a job, this won't get it for you. If you're in rehearsal or performance, it is the director's place to give suggestions. If you have ideas or suggestions, talk privately to the director or the stage manager; leave the other actors alone.

As hundreds of new people enter the acting field each year, a growing concern has been expressed that professional standards are breaking down. This does not imply that newcomers are the sole violators of the theater's rules and traditions. Often, they are not.

As an actor, you will be held in the same regard in which you hold yourself.

5

What About Agents?

Do you really need an agent to have a successful career? Most performers believe having an agent is more important in Los Angeles than in New York, but in any case, you should always remember that an agent cannot get you a job. You must do that yourself.

An agent submits you for jobs, arranges the appointments or necessary interviews, negotiates your salary and other conditions, and receives a percentage of your earnings (a commission) if you get the job. Actually, this description is oversimplified, for a good agent does much more.

Agents function importantly in theater, motion pictures, and television, and within these fields, their business relationships with actors are regulated by Equity, SAG, and AFTRA. Such regulation is made possible by the issuance to agents of franchises; for example, an agent cannot represent any member of SAG unless the Screen Actors Guild has issued a franchise to that agent. Most agents are franchised by all three unions, which means that they have agreed to abide by the rules and conditions established by each.

But some agents may hold franchises from only one or two of the unions. This is especially true in California, where theatrical activity is subordinate to television and film production; thus, a number of agents in Hollywood do not hold Equity franchises but function actively in the motion picture and television fields.

Do You Need an Agent?

Whether an actor needs an agent is the subject of some disagreement among people in the business. It is important to understand that there is a difference between being sent for an interview in Hollywood and for live theater in New York (where, with enough luck and persistence, an actor can often get an interview without being sent by an agent). Still, as previously pointed out, the actor sent by an agent has a specific appointment and usually gets the interview with the person he or she has been sent to see. In Hollywood, you can't walk past the guard at the studio gate and into the casting office without an appointment—not even to see the receptionist. It is probably true that if you can get a reputable agent interested in you, you are better off. But this does not mean that you should sign a contract with that agent right away. The agent who signs you without first having seen your work is probably not the one you'll want when your career gets off the ground. Wait, and if you get a chance and are seen to advantage, you may be able to take your choice of agents.

Exclusive Management or Freelance?

The unions have several types of contracts and authorizations under which agents and actors do business together. But essentially, an actor either is a "freelance" performer or that actor has an exclusive contract with a single agent.

If you are freelance, which means that you aren't signed exclusively to one agent, you are not committed to have an agent represent you exclusively in a particular field. If an agent submits you for a film and you get it, he or she gets a commission for that film. If another agent gets you a part in another movie, that agent gets the commission for that film. You don't have to be signed to an agent to have the agent represent you for a particular job. Many agents and actors work together without exclusive contracts on a trial basis. If a freelance actor is submitted for a job by a particular agent, the actor merely signs an authorization that specifies that the agent represents her or him for that job and sets forth the commission to be paid if he or she gets the role. This is the way most young actors work when they first begin their careers. Some established performers work this way, too. It's a good way for an actor and an agent to get to know each other. But under no circumstances should the actor be submitted for the same job by more than one agent. The actor must make sure this doesn't happen.

Each union authorizes an exclusive management contract that applies only to its jurisdiction. If you sign with one agent, you cannot approach other agents to submit you for parts in that field, and you should refer all applicable offers of employment to the agent with whom you are signed. Usually, these exclusive management contracts are for periods of from one to three years, with provisions for termination if you don't work in the applicable jurisdiction within a reasonable length of time.

Although it is not necessary to sign with an agent to have the agent work for you, some actors and some agents prefer it. To the agent, it means that there is less likelihood of devoting time and effort to your career only to have you become famous—largely through her or his efforts—and then leave just when the agent's commission is beginning to mean something. For the actor, the exclusive management contract implies that the agent takes a long-range interest in developing the actor's career, will help with advice and legal problems, and will fight for the best possible conditions and salary. If you are lucky enough to get a good agent, this can be a great factor in furthering your career.

Unhappily, it can work the other way, too. Some agencies, including the very biggest, have been known to sign well-known actors to exclusive management contracts and then sit back and do nothing, secure in the knowledge that whatever work the actors get because of their own stature in the profession, the agency will still get its commission.

There is no simple answer to the question of exclusive representation, which is why the choice of an agent is so important. One thing is sure: the agent and the actor must trust each other; don't sign an exclusive contract with an agent you don't trust. Other actors and unions are a good source of advice on this score. At any rate, this is not the kind of decision that newcomers customarily have to face.

Incidentally, it is possible to have one agent represent you exclusively for films (by virtue of signing a SAG contract) and to have another represent you for television (on a separate AFTRA contract); or to be represented exclusively in one medium and freelance in others. In my view, this situation is not especially desirable, except for theater work, where it is quite common: many actors have exclusive contracts with agents for films and television and then freelance insofar as the stage is concerned. This is perfectly proper, as long as there is no misunderstanding.

Why Is It Important to Deal with Franchised Agents?

Screen Actors Guild has posted the following information on its website. Legitimate talent agencies do not charge a fee payable in advance for registering you, or for résumés, for public relations services, for screen tests, for photographs, for acting lessons, or for many other services used to separate you from your money. If you are signed as a client by a legitimate talent agency, you will pay that agency nothing until you work. Nothing in advance. Legitimate talent agencies normally do not advertise for clients in newspaper classified columns, nor do they solicit through the mail. If a purported talent agent seeks to send you to a particular photographer for pictures, hold your wallet tightly and run for the nearest exit. Chances are the agent is a phony and receives a cut of the photographer's fee. If you need photographs, choose your own photographer, and try another agent—one who is franchised by the performer unions.

Franchised agents have agreed to comply with the conditions and codes of professional ethics embodied in their contracts with the unions. Most of them do. Indeed, many agents truly take great pride in discovering and promoting new talent and in helping to build careers through wise and experienced counsel. Such persons are invaluable to an actor and are worth far more than the percentage they actually get paid. But not every agent is so dedicated, and the franchise is designed to ensure protection against the agent who perpetually tries to pirate other agents' clients, who uses an actor's need to work as a basis for making personal demands, who overcharges on commissions or tries to collect payment even when not entitled to it, or who withholds salary or indulges in other shady practices. There are agents who do these things. How do they get away with it? Such malpractice is possible only when the actors involved do not understand their rights or are too intimidated to report infractions to the unions. The agent who is interested only in a "fast buck" is not the one with whom you want to stay. Under no circumstances should you enter into an exclusive management agreement with such a person. This type of agent is a menace to actors, to other agents, and to the entire profession.

One thing to remember: an agent who holds franchises from the unions may represent you even if you're not a union member. But a union member may not work through an agent not franchised by her or his union. Even if you are not a union member, stay pretty close to the franchised agents. It won't do you much good to be handled by someone who doesn't represent professionals. AFTRA, Equity, and SAG print lists of agents they franchise, and these lists are available from the union offices.

In addition, the agency rules of each union are published in booklet form; when you join a union, you should ask for these rules and study them. Not only do the rules protect you, but you also have certain obligations that you must fulfill. Understanding the agency rules of your unions can save you a lot of grief. Each union has an executive who handles agency affairs. When you have questions of any kind, check with this individual.

How Much Do You Pay?

You never pay more than 10 percent of your salary to any agent franchised by a union in any circumstances, whether you are working in films, television, or theater. There are no exceptions. Even if, by some unique turn of events, two agents have arranged to "split commission" on a job—as sometimes happens when New York and

Hollywood agents arrange to represent the same clients in different locations—the most the actor can pay is 10 percent. This kind of dual representation is not something you are going to be concerned with at the start of your career. If you can manage to negotiate with an agent to accept a smaller percentage, that's all to the good, for the commissions specified in the franchise agreements are maximum payments, and actors may pay less. Usually, however, commission percentage is standard, except for high-salaried stars whose earnings and overhead (they also need attorneys, accountants, and secretaries) are relatively high. If you get an agent, you will probably pay the maximum commission.

Television

In the normal course of business, AFTRA does not permit payment of commission to an agent if such payment will reduce the performer's take-home pay below the union's minimum salary. There are some exceptions that permit payment of an agent's commission on scale (union minimum) wages, but when in doubt, you should check with the union's agency department or the AFTRA Local office. Very often, employers arrange to pay salaries equal to scale plus commission, so that both the actor and the agent will comply with the AFTRA rule. Of course, if you are earning well over scale, you pay the agent up to 10 percent of your gross salary.

These arrangements apply whether you are freelance or under an exclusive management contract.

Films

At this writing, SAG and the agents' organization have not signed a new franchise agreement, but actors are continuing to be represented by their agents when they work in SAG's jurisdiction.

Theater

Here again, Equity's rules are different and more complicated. For work in the theater, there are two types of contracts between actor and agent: the agency authorization contract for a specific engagement and the exclusive management contract, which may cover your employment in the entire legitimate theater industry, or which may be limited to one or more specific engagements.

In both cases, salaries of less than $396.00 a week are not commissionable. On salaries between $397.00 and $498.50, there is a one-time fee of $100.00. For salaries of more than $498.50 a week, there is a 5 percent commission for the rehearsal period (at minimum) and a 10 percent commission during public performance.

Things to Remember

Even if you are a freelance actor, never play agents off each other. If one agent calls you for a job and another has already approached you about the same job, tell them both exactly what the situation is. Unfortunately, actors most often get in trouble by not wanting to say "no" to anybody, for fear of losing employment. But you'll get a bad reputation that way.

Also, be absolutely sure that you and the agent understand each other before you see about the job he or she sends you on. In other words, you don't have your house painted first and discuss the price afterward. The same things hold true of your relationships with agents. Usually, the maximum payments authorized by the unions apply to each job, but not always. Agree on payment before the agent starts to work, bearing in mind that you can never pay more than the maximum amounts specified by the unions.

Don't trust an agent who claims to have exclusive casting rights to anything. Some agents are paid to function as casting consultants, but in these circumstances, they are never allowed to take commission from the salary of an actor who works in that particular show. There is no question that in the past, certain agents (very few, incidentally) have made a practice of finding out from producers which actors are under consideration for a particular role, then calling these actors and informing them that to work in the production, they must be submitted by the agent in question. As a result, many performers who would rather work through agents who have already helped them are afraid to refuse this illegal "exclusive" representation. Such cases should be immediately reported to the proper union; you will be protected and the agent will, in all likelihood, lose her or his franchise.

Actors who do not honor their contracts with agents can also cause a good deal of trouble. The unions take a dim view of actors who play one agent against another, and the actor who does this quite often incurs unwelcome publicity and an unsavory reputation.

The main thing to remember, as you start to make the rounds, is that agents need you as much as you need them. You should expect to be treated with courtesy and candor. If you want an agent, there are many of them in business, and there is one who is right for you. But remember, the lack of an agent has never kept a brilliant talent from being recognized.

The unions provide lists of franchised agents. In addition, *Back Stage* periodically publishes lists of franchised agents. *Ross Reports* contains detailed agency information, noting if the agency is franchised, type of clients it specializes in (children, voice-overs, theater, and so forth), and its policy on accepting photos, résumés, and tapes. *Ross Reports* publishes lists for both New York and Los Angeles.

Personal Managers

The unions do not have formal relationships with "personal" or "business" managers. That doesn't mean they are bad; it just means that they are not "franchised" by the unions. There are many well-established firms engaged in personal and/or business management. However, such firms usually handle established or well-known artists, and they neither advertise for newcomers nor promise employment.

Personal managers are not franchised by the unions, nor are they subject to regulations that apply to agents. Therefore, they may collect fees as high as the traffic will bear. In turn, they should provide more comprehensive services than agents, acting sometimes also as business managers and financial and legal advisers. They may invest considerable time and effort on your behalf, but you should proceed with caution before signing any agreements.

Independent Casting Directors

Casting consultants are employed by studios, networks, advertising agencies, or producers. They are paid by these companies and not by the people they hire. They, too, are not bound by any union restrictions. *Ross Reports* carries a list of independent casting directors on both coasts.

Some Words of Warning

Many people, lured by the glamorous lifestyle and the promise of high salaries, have been victimized by false promises of money and stardom. Here, as in all walks of life, it is necessary to be an informed consumer about any agreement you make in seeking to further your career.

An acquaintance of mine with knowledge of show business recently received in the mail a letter informing him that his son, age four, had been brought to the attention of a personal management firm specializing in children for commercials and modeling. He was asked to call for an appointment so that one of their "agents" could see the child personally. On the evening of the appointment, an "agent" came to the house and began by saying that the chances of a child actually appearing in a commercial are not good, but that this particular child was so "perfect" for commercials that for a deposit of only $185 to cover photo expenses and mailings, the "agent" would have his firm issue an option for the child that would run for five years. The money, he said, could be paid in installments or even by postdated check. It turned out, after some investigation, that the Federal Trade Commission was aware of this organization, and that it was merely a front for a photo firm. Unfortunately, this true story is not an isolated case. So beware!

Some things to watch out for in dealing with an agent or personal manager are:

• The phony ad in newspapers or trade journals that says "new faces wanted" for commercials, modeling, or movies, adding that "no experience is necessary." These ads also appear in the help-wanted columns of newspapers and often print alluring salary ranges. Most, if not all, of such ads are come-ons.

• The company name that sounds similar to the name of a well-known movie studio, television network, or other established and reputable organization. This is used to give the false impression that the two are connected.

• The "agent" who obtains lists of children's names from unsuspecting teachers, or waits outside schools or playgrounds to solicit children.

• The agent who asks for a fee in advance. A "registration fee" paid to any agent or personal manager is always a worthless investment. This is the main characteristic that distinguishes a legitimate talent agency from a phony one. Legitimate agents and personal managers work on a commission basis. They don't get any money unless and until you get paid for doing the work they have obtained for you.

• The agent or manager who may insist that you take acting lessons at a particular school or from a particular teacher, or who tries to arrange for you to buy expensive photographs, audition tapes, or other services or materials sold by someone he or she suggests. Perhaps you will be given a test (asked to read a scene or a commercial) and told that you have "a lot of talent," but that it needs to be developed. Then the agent will try to send you to a school run by an associate.

• The office of the agent or manager who displays photos of famous stars to give the impression that they are represented by the agent, when, in fact, they are not.

• You may be asked to sign a contract full of confusing legal language. This will bind you, but will let the phony agent off the hook.

• The location and name of phony agencies may frequently change because they go out of business to avoid prosecution, only to turn up later under another name at another address. Reputable businesses should have a fixed address. If, during normal business hours, nobody answers the phone, be careful.

A swindle of another nature was reported in the press not long ago. It involved a sophisticated telephone scam to bilk aspiring actors out of hundreds of dollars. It worked like this: Notices were posted with modeling agencies announcing the need for non-union extras to work in a new film starring, variously, Patrick Swayze, Rob Lowe, or Arnold Schwarzenegger. A fictitious producer and production studio was named, along with a phone number that led to a recording. After an actor left his or her number, someone posing as a movie producer returned the call and told the actor, after a brief conversation, that he or she would be perfect for a role in the film. However, the actor must first talk to a Screen Actors Guild representative. The actor was then instructed to wire $150 to $400 for union dues to a fictitious Screen Actors Guild official in Hollywood or New York. Once the money was sent, neither the "producer" nor the "SAG official" was ever heard from again.

SAG attorneys received complaints from victims in cities throughout the United States, including Chicago, Louisville, Milwaukee, Toledo, Memphis, Amarillo, Phoenix, San Diego, and San Francisco. The scam always occurred on weekends, when no one could call a SAG office to check out the offer.

Screen Actors Guild never takes money up front. Applicants must visit an office and fill out forms. SAG further cautions all actors to be careful; never send money up front for anything—an agent, a manager, or a job. Legitimate businesses don't operate that way.

6

SCHOOL DAZE

MOST PERFORMERS—EVEN stars—study, work out, and keep in shape because in the final analysis, the only product they have to offer is themselves. Prior to a recent Broadway appearance, an Academy Award–winning actress rehearsed up to seven hours and ran several miles a day to improve her breath control and her endurance.

"Learning should never stop," a well-known director told a graduating class of a prominent drama school a few years ago. "Every master carpenter sharpens his tools regularly while he is looking for work and even more regularly while he is on the job." Actors have always studied. But the necessity for constant training is even greater today than ever before, for the virtual disappearance of the old-time stock companies has deprived us of an important source of on-the-job training, and the growing popularity of the musical play has made versatility increasingly necessary. Today, almost all dancers also sing; almost all singers dance and act, and many young actors of serious purpose work to perfect their abilities at all three. A Labor Department survey conducted several years ago showed that most professional performers spent up to fourteen hours a week studying or training from nine to twelve months a year. They also spent more than several thousand dollars a year to finance this training. There is no reason to think that things have changed.

The advantages of a college education are as obvious in the acting profession as they are anywhere else: a broadening of knowledge, the development of personality, and a deeper appreciation of culture and its importance in life. In college, you have to take subjects such as English literature, sociology, mathematics, languages—the things that may end up feeding you and your family at an unexpected time. For these reasons, and because the competition for good jobs in every field is so intense, a college education is increasingly important. The history of the theater, the study of plays and traditions, the exposure to all dramatic forms and backgrounds—these are offered only in college, and knowledge of them creates greater opportunity for diversified theatrical activity. The actors who also function as successful directors, writers, designers, and producers are the ones who know more about their business than just acting.

Additionally, theater classes taken in college are important for two reasons: they give the student broad general knowledge, and they provide hands-on experience and skills that can be valuable in a number of careers. In short, a theater degree can be important both for students committed to a career in theater and to those interested in other areas that require communication skills, such as public relations or sales. It is also likely that even someone highly committed to a career in theater will have to seek other employment at some time during his or her career, either permanently or for "survival."

It has been said that there are two types of jobs: "professional work" that requires special training, such as law and medicine; and "trait-oriented work," for which an employer looks for special traits, such as communication skills, imagination, reasoning ability, and judgment. Theater training can be valuable for many careers that fall into the second category.

Skills and personality traits that can be developed as a result of theater-training classes include: oral communication skills, creative problem-solving abilities, a willingness to work cooperatively, initiative, promptness and respect for deadlines, ability to learn quickly, adaptability, ability to work under pressure, acceptance of disappointment, self-discipline, concentration, leadership skills, and self-confidence.

Once again, *Dramatics* magazine can be very helpful. It publishes an annual college theater directory, with profiles and audition information on scores of schools throughout the country. Each entry contains information about scholarships, admission requirements, auditions, deadline dates, and program characteristics. *Dramatics* is published monthly except in June, July, and August by the Educational Theater Association, 2343 Auburn Avenue, Cincinnati, Ohio 45219.

Choosing a School

Today many colleges and universities have professional theater groups on their campuses. This offers a unique opportunity to work in a professional company with professional actors and directors, while at the same time obtaining a degree and pursuing other areas of study. The Huntington Theater Company at Boston University, the Pioneer Theater Company at the University of Utah, Yale University, McCarter Theater at Princeton University, and Syracuse

Stage at Syracuse University are but a few of the college-based professional theaters operating throughout the country.

An organization called University/Resident Theatre Association, Inc. (U/RTA) negotiates with Actors' Equity for wages and working conditions for professional actors to work with students in university theaters. Members of U/RTA include: University of Alabama, University of Arizona, Florida State University, University of Minnesota, Northwestern University, Purdue University, and University of Wisconsin, among more than twenty-five others. Contact U/RTA at 1560 Broadway, Suite 903, New York, New York 10036.

Information on college and university theaters can also be obtained from the National Association of Schools of Theater at 11250 Roger Bacon Drive, Suite 21, Reston, Virginia 22090. This association is comprised of approximately 140 schools, primarily at the collegiate level, but also some precollegiate and community schools of theater. It is the national accrediting agency for theater and theater-related disciplines. It publishes a directory each spring, containing lists of accredited schools and all of the programs and degrees offered.

Choosing the right school is important. First, as with any course of study, you must decide if you want a small school or a large one, urban or rural, close to home or out of town. More specifically, if you are planning to study theater, do you want a concentration in theater, or do you want a liberal arts education coupled with an opportunity to take some theater courses? After making the initial decisions, it will be necessary to examine both the faculty and the curriculum. Who on the faculty is currently working professionally? Do they bring in guest directors and other personnel? Is there an opportunity to work with a professional theater during the school year? How many productions will you be involved in during the school year? Is there an alumni network? What are recent graduates doing? How many are currently working in theater?

Actor Hume Cronyn in his autobiography, *A Terrible Liar: A Memoir*, said this about training:

> I believe it is desirable to have it. You can of course get by—even prosper—without it, but if your schooling gives you no more than a rudimentary sense of your instrument—the control of your body, voice, the power of your imagination, perhaps even a peek into your own soul—then you've made a fortunate start.

College theater is one of the last proving grounds left to the actor—one of the few places where he or she is still able to learn by trial and error, to make mistakes, and then to correct them without bearing an additional burden of fear for a job, family security, and a future as a performer.

But a college education alone does not offer enough straight acting training. Rather, it is the first step in the endless process of study. After college, one needs to study acting with a teacher or at a school that concentrates on acting and acting only. (This kind of training should be undertaken after college, not in place of it.) While college offers the wide spectrum of exposure and experience to give the beginning actor a broad frame of reference, it does not usually prepare the student of acting for the competitive reality of professional theater. Playing before a perpetually friendly and uncritical audience in the company of others who have never been subject to commercial pressures is a safe but professionally unrealistic experience.

Not too long ago, a survey taken of twenty-four Broadway singers and dancers showed that more than one-third went to college, one-fourth spoke a foreign language fluently, and almost all attended weekly singing, acting, and dancing classes.

Let's assume you've finished college and are ready to continue your study of acting. What next? Naturally, the big centers of commercial theater—New York, Los Angeles, and Chicago—offer the widest choice, since most actors congregate in these cities, and many teachers also work as actors or directors.

How do you find out where you should study? Perusal of the telephone book or examination of the ads placed in trade papers can be a confusing experience. Literally hundreds of teachers and schools vie for your hard-earned dollar. Some of them are scams; others, while sincere, offer nothing of significant value; some may be too highly specialized to suit your particular needs; others may work in a manner alien to your personality. But you can be sure that there will be several that can help you sharpen and perfect your talent.

You will get no list of recommended schools from the actors' unions. They can't and won't endorse specific teachers. In choosing a school or teacher, it is well to consider the people who teach there and what their experience has been. Also, try to find out who has studied there recently and what they have to say about it. Other actors are a good source of information. So is the school itself. As a prospective customer, you should shop carefully, and you should never enroll in a school without first having had an interview with a member of its staff. Don't be afraid to ask what that school has to offer. Also, you have a right to sit in on a class before enrolling. Find out for yourself how the teachers work, and see what you think of it.

Some schools offer a complete curriculum, including acting, dance, voice, and speech. Whether you want to study all these things at once depends upon the extent of your available time and money. Some people can afford only one course at a time. Don't let this discourage you. Assuming you have a qualified teacher, you'll get as much out of your one course as you put into it. Actually, you may be better off by starting out with a single course; you may later decide that you don't like the school and want to change.

Acting Classes

School and class are good places to meet people with whom you may work or want to work later in your career. Well-known film, television, and Broadway actress Swoosie Kurtz described her experience in a seminar at Actors' Equity:

> I was lucky enough to attend the London Academy of Music and Dramatic Arts (LAMDA). I was a complete Anglophile and was dying to go to English drama school. They were the first people I auditioned for, and I got accepted and went there for almost two years. The only bad thing was I should have listened to my mom, who wanted me to go to Yale. I had a full scholarship to the University of Southern California and left after two years because I didn't really see the point. I wanted to do acting all day long. In retrospect, I should have gone to Yale because I think I would have gotten to places a lot quicker because of the network—which is not a dirty word. I used to think, oh, that's politics and connections and knowing people and all that stuff—and it's not. Other people are what it is all about. If I would have gone to Yale, I would have gotten to meet playwright Chris Durang and Meryl Streep and Sigourney Weaver and all these people, instead of ultimately working with them later on, which I was lucky enough to do. But I would have known them from the start. Instead, I came to New York cold after being in drama school in London for two years. They didn't know me and I didn't know them, and I really had to start from scratch.

The late actor Christopher Reeve said much the same thing in an interview for *Equity News*:

My first move, when I came to New York, was to get connected with teachers who were well respected . . . I think you want to meet people who are connected. That's the strategy that I would probably use if I were starting out again. There is so much going on it is very tempting not to train properly. You can be eighteen or nineteen years old, and somebody can call you and offer you a movie. An otherwise serious actor suddenly gives up on his training and goes to cash in on the fact the people want him now. But just because they want you now doesn't mean they're going to want you in four or five years. I would not want to be one of those actors who has not thought about the future, or trained. What happens to those people when they're twenty-five or more? It is also important to plan your career properly. There are some chances to get ahead of yourself, to get opportunities that you're not really ready for. So I think if you get ahead of yourself and you suddenly get chances you're not ready for, it can be as much of a problem as spending ten years thinking, 'When is the phone going to ring?'

Acting classes may cost several hundred dollars per course; individual instruction may be much higher. Only in rare instances, such as coaching for a specific part, is individual instruction more valuable than class work. On the contrary, working with a group can be the more valuable, since acting demands the presence of other people both onstage and in the audience. Most singers and dancers spend more than $100 a week on classes.

Even after careful inquiry, you may find that the school in which you've enrolled is not for you. This is not unusual; the relationship between teacher and student is a very personal thing, and there are many different approaches to teaching and acting. It's quite probable that a certain method can help you during one stage of your development and do nothing for you at another. There is no sure way to avoid mistakes in choosing your first school or teacher, and even if you land in the wrong place for a while, it's seldom a totally wasted experience.

There are certain dangers, however, that should be avoided:

• Never enroll in a school that guarantees to get you an acting job, a union card, or an agent. No school can do these things, and this kind of representation is downright dishonest. I have never seen a reputable school or teacher advertise in this manner.

• Never succumb to the "teacher" who tells you that "for a fee, I can arrange a showcase so that you'll be seen," or who promises "a screen test." Hundreds of gullible young actors fall for this routine every year, and none of them has ever landed a job as a result.

• Be suspicious of teachers who do not have legitimate credentials and who claim to produce television shows, movies, or theatrical productions. Verify the claims before signing contracts for lessons or paying cash to anyone.

• Fraudulent training schools often advertise using photos of former students whom the school claims to have placed in high-paying entertainment jobs. Like phony agents, these kinds of schools may demand exorbitant registration fees for worthless instruction and demand that you have photographs taken by their photographers.

• In the case of fly-by-night acting schools, classes often don't begin on schedule and sometimes will not begin at all. Suddenly, the "school" or "teacher" will disappear and can no longer be reached by telephone. If and when classes actually do begin, they may consist of little more than the student reading over and over from a script and being assured by the "teacher" that there is improvement.

If you have any doubts about the school in which you're interested, feel free to check its references with the unions. Although they cannot express a preference for particular schools with respect to the quality of instruction, these organizations certainly can tell you whether the advertising is ethical or whether their members have complained of misrepresentation.

Actors' Equity has begun a program of outreach to students in an effort to inform them about the union and better prepare them for a career in theater. At this writing, the coordinator of the program is Amy Dolan, who accepted the position after completing an acting assignment. On stage since the age of seven, Ms. Dolan appeared on Broadway, toured in Europe, and worked in numerous regional theater productions. She also worked in commercials. In addition, she started a summer theater camp for kids interested in musical theater and produced a series of seminars on "How to Treat Your Dream like a Business" and other related subjects.

Ms. Dolan says a well-rounded education is always valuable. Also, for acting, studying at a conservatory can be most worthwhile.

7

GOING FOR IT!

ARE YOU STILL convinced that acting is the career for you? Do you really want to "go for it"? Do you have the drive and stamina to pursue your passion for acting given the hardships you may have to endure? If so, read on.

Christopher Reeve said that he had painted houses and "done all those things you need to do to keep money coming in. I was persistent, but I never wanted to do anything other than act. I don't think being an actor is a decision you can make in a rational way. You don't say, 'I think I really might try being an actor, but if I don't do that, I could just as easily work in a bank.' It's not an either/or proposition. I think people who are actors really have to be actors. What I hate to see are people who are playing at 'Well, maybe I'll be an actor.'"

The best way to explain the employment rate for actors is to illustrate the unemployment rate, which, it is generally agreed, hovers around 85 percent. So, while the general public hears mostly about swimming pools, luxury cars, and multi-million-dollar deals, only a very small percentage of performers actually achieve these things. More often than not, between jobs as performers, they are either unemployed or working outside their profession.

Theodore Bikel, former president of Equity, often regretted that he seemed, at times, to be presiding over an association of people "many of whom are sometime-actors and full-time waiters and cab drivers."

Despite the odds, the ranks of actors continue to increase annually.

The bulk of commercial activity calling for actors' services is in New York and Los Angeles. Of course, there are many hundreds of jobs available in other places throughout the country (with some significant concentration in Chicago), but most film and theatrical production emanates from the coasts. Paradoxically, however, this does not mean that your career will profit from an immediate invasion of Broadway or Hollywood. We know about the fierce competition in these places. We know, too, that a fish that goes unnoticed in the ocean may be important in a pond.

Opportunities for talent often lie outside the major production centers, and many actors have created careers in their own communities, often making impressive reputations for themselves as hosts of local television programs; as leading players in regional theater groups; and as disc jockeys, radio announcers, local radio personalities, and on public access cable television. The same energy and persistence that it takes to land a job in films or on Broadway might, if concentrated in your own community, establish a flourishing professional theater. The trend in show business is more and more toward decentralization—toward establishment of state and regional theaters throughout the country. In this direction lies considerable opportunity and challenge.

We know that many well-known television personalities who now have their own network programs began their careers by working as announcers, disc jockeys, or commentators on television or radio stations in their hometowns, and that many well-known actors began by working with local stock companies or in regional theaters.

Regional Theaters

Regional theaters are generally established to serve a specific community with productions of artistic excellence and affordable cost. These theaters usually have more professional standards than some community-based amateur theaters, and the actors who work in them consider acting a vocation rather than an avocation. Regional professional theater has become an important influence in American theater.

Theatre Communications Group (TCG) is the national service organization for nonprofit professional theater. It was founded in 1961 to provide a national forum and communications network for the then-emerging nonprofit theaters, and to respond to the needs of theaters and theater artists for centralized services. TCG serves theaters, artists, administrators, and technicians through casting and referral services, publications, conferences and seminars, and other programs. Two of its publications are particularly helpful: *American Theatre* magazine, which contains important theater news, along with listings of productions at all its member regional theaters; and *ArtSEARCH*, the National Employment Service bulletin.

For performers, TCG has national auditions, which provide a unique opportunity for graduating acting students from university theater departments and professional training programs to demonstrate their talent before directors and producers of nonprofit professional theaters throughout the United States. TCG publishes an auditions directory of participating students to provide theaters with a guide for future hiring as well. In addition, TCG has a casting information service, maintains files of qualified actors, makes casting suggestions, and provides the consultant service of a staff of professional casting directors. TCG also maintains the only fully professional service specializing in placing directors, designers, stage managers, technical personnel, literary managers, and administrators in theater-related jobs. TCG's more than two hundred constituent and associate member theaters include the Guthrie Theater in Minneapolis, Actors Theatre of Louisville, Milwaukee Repertory Theater Company, Seattle Repertory Theatre, and the American Conservatory Theater in San Francisco. TCG is located at 520 Eighth Avenue, New York, New York 10018.

Opportunities for Minorities and Women

While employment in the performing arts fields is, at best, sporadic and difficult to find, the situation is worse for minority groups, women, and senior citizens.

All of the performer unions have committees specifically concerned with employment of minorities, women, and the disabled. Unions and management in all media meet regularly to assess the employment situation and recommend and implement improvements. Several of the unions also have equal employment business representatives on staff to administer and enforce affirmative action policies.

The Interguild Committee of Performers with Disabilities maintains an office in Hollywood and has successfully staged several showcases for performers. It also conducts workshops for disabled performers. A similar committee is at work in New York under the auspices of the performer unions.

The Non-Traditional Casting Project is an organization that grew out of Actors' Equity Association into a separate entity; it maintains extensive files of minority and disabled performers. The NTCP is located at 165 West Forty-Sixth Street, New York, New York 10036.

Related Fields

Many successful directors, writers, producers, stage managers, and choreographers were once actors. Some still are. The more actors know about everything connected with their business, the better are their chances of making a living.

"Being broke is very boring," successful actor Conard Fowkes reminds us. "It is essential that the actor be able to survive financially."

Since the best way to obtain employment is to create it yourself, this might mean starting your own theater, as was done by Margo Jones (Dallas), Zelda Fichandler (Washington, D.C.), and Nina Vance (Houston).

Even in large production centers, actors and actresses may earn a substantial portion of their incomes as models. Many dancers, singers, and performers also teach. I know one young dancer whose knowledge of French is superb. Although she works as a dancer, 80 percent of her income last year was earned by giving French lessons. Two friends, both female singers, earned most of their income last year performing on cruise ships.

My present occupation is editing and writing, at which I have managed for many years to make a living. Why? Because when I was acting, I majored in journalism in college; I still acted, but I also started to direct, teach, and write. I didn't plan my present career, but by the time I wanted to quit the business of performing, I had acquired other skills for which people were willing to pay.

One actress I know edits a magazine, teaches computer programming, and works for a medical organization where (thanks to her acting talents) she portrays patients whose symptoms paramedics are supposed to diagnose. Another performer has organized a small company that offers escorted tours of her city's offbeat attractions to people attending conventions. She arranged a tie-in with an airline and gradually expanded to the point where she was able to offer work to others in the business. Another talented actress, who wanted to be more active and stay in Minneapolis, organized a successful modeling agency and managed to do both.

The Actors' Work Program has records of actors who have received counseling and tuition grants and gone on to successful careers in nursing, financial consulting, real estate, fashion designing, catering, social work, teaching, and a host of other careers. Many of those who have successfully made the transition into new careers or found fulfillment in supplementary careers say their background and experience as performers was very helpful to them in their new professions.

Branching out in these ways requires an understanding of business problems and methods, which brings us back to the fact that a well-rounded education is important.

Temporary Work

So, you've decided acting is your passion and you must pursue your dream—no matter what. But you will have to support yourself while you are "making the rounds." Temporary employment is the way to go, and there may be temporary employment agencies and temporary jobs advertised in the newspapers or on the Internet. *Backstage* and *Backstage West* carry many advertisements from temporary employment agencies. The challenge is to find work that is flexible, somewhat lucrative, and not too boring. Some actors prefer a long-term temp situation; others like to change jobs frequently. Some people are partial to the night shift; others manage to work auditions into their daily work schedule.

The biggest minus to temping is qualifying for health insurance. Today, some agencies are offering health insurance to longtime, "regular" employees. You can check this out when signing up. They may also offer paid vacation days after working a certain number of hours.

You should register with a lot of employment services to increase your chances of finding work and then follow up with phone calls. Computer skills are extremely valuable. Some actors say that getting a job as a temp is similar to getting a job in acting—it's who you know. A friend on the job might be able to recommend you if an opening comes up. And if office work doesn't appeal to you, there's always waiting on tables, or even sales. But it's all just until you get your "big break."

8

NORTHERN EXPOSURE

AT THIS WRITING, many movies and television shows are filmed in other countries, especially Canada. Broadway shows also have opened in Canada before moving to New York. It is also necessary to belong to a labor union to work in many areas.

Canadian Actors' Equity Association

Canadian Actors' Equity Association (CAEA) is the professional organization of performers, directors, choreographers, and stage managers in Canada who are engaged in English-language live performance, including the stage, opera, ballet, and dance.

Equity in Canada was founded in 1955 as a branch of Actors' Equity in the United States, and an amicable separation was achieved in 1976. Administration and governing of the union is similar to that of Actors' Equity in the United States. Leaders of the two unions meet regularly to oversee smooth working transitions from country to country.

How to Join

There are two ways to become a member of CAEA. The first is by signing an Equity contract. Also, a member of another performing arts union or association in Canada or in the United States must become a member of CAEA to work in a theater that operates under Equity's jurisdiction. The principle is that a performer can't be a professional in one part of the business and a nonprofessional in another. Membership may also be secured through a recognized apprenticeship program. An acting apprentice must complete three shows for two different companies in a three-year period. A stage manager apprentice must complete six shows for two different companies, or eight shows for one company, in a three-year period. Then the apprentice has six months in which to join CAEA.

Dues and Initiation Fees

If a person joins Equity via contract, the initiation fee is $750. Under the apprentice method, the apprentice pays $125 per show as an acting apprentice, or $62.50 per show as a stage management apprentice, to a limit of $300. These apprentice fees are credited to the initiation fee when the apprentice becomes a member. If joining as a member of another union, a member may deduct the amount paid as an initiation fee to a maximum of 50 percent of CAEA's initiation fee.

Basic dues are $135 per year. In addition to the basic dues, members pay 2 percent of their contractual weekly fees up to a maximum of $1,050 per calendar year.

Membership Benefits

Canadian Actors' Equity Association administers a registered retirement savings plan and an accident and sickness insurance plan for members; places travel insurance for all members; records contracts and ensures that they correspond to the agreements; and guarantees that every member is bonded so that if a theater closes, members will receive a termination fee plus any other monies owing. In addition, CAEA has an Equity e-drive mailing list that carries information about auditions and other opportunities, is updated daily, and publishes a regular newsletter.

CAEA has two offices: The national office is at 44 Victoria Street, Toronto, Ontario M5C 3C4; telephone: (416) 867-9165; fax: (416) 867-9246. There is also a western office at 505321 Water Street, Vancouver, British Columbia V6B 1B8; telephone: (604) 682-6173; fax: (604) 682-6174.

Alliance of Canadian Cinema, Television, and Radio Artists

The Alliance of Canadian Cinema, Television, and Radio Artists (ACTRA) represents performers in the recorded media, from television scenes, commercials, and radio dramas to movies-of-the-week and feature films. It is the equivalent of both the Screen Actors Guild and the American Federation of Television and Radio Artists in the United States.

How to Join

There are five steps to becoming a full ACTRA member:

1. Get cast in a speaking role in a film/series/movie-of-the-week or a silent on camera (SOC) role in a commercial.
2. Buy a work permit from the ACTRA membership department and indicate that you want to join the apprenticeship program. Pay an initiation fee, attend an

apprentice members' meeting, and receive an apprentice member's card.

3. Accumulate five additional paid work permits (or two additional permits if you are a visible minority or disabled) for roles other than background/stand-in roles.

4. When you purchase your sixth work permit (or third, in the case of minority/disability status), inform the ACTRA membership department that you wish to become a full member.

5. Attend a full members' meeting and receive your ACTRA member's card.

What Does It Cost?

Apprentice members pay $30 per year and fees for subsequent work permits that vary according to the role. Full members pay basic dues of $175 per year plus 2 percent of gross earnings (up to a maximum of $3,000). Insurance premiums are paid by the producer, while retirement benefits are shared between producer and performer. Apprentice members pay a $75 initiation fee plus fees for each of the work permits they require. For detailed information, visit the website at actratoronto.com.

Membership Benefits

ACTRA negotiates and administers agreements with producers, studios, television, radio, and cable networks. It ensures members have a safe work environment; makes sure members are paid for both their work and the future use of their image; administers an insurance and retirement plan for members; and provides training and professional development opportunities.

ACTRA's main office is at 625 Church Street, Toronto, Ontario M4Y 2G1; telephone: (416) 928-2278 or toll-free (877) 913-2278.

Runaway Production

At this writing, a source of major concern in the U.S. film and television industries is "runaway production"—the loss of revenue and jobs due to favorable money exchange rates, lower costs, and—extremely important—foreign governments' tax incentives. Runaway production is similar to the "outsourcing" of jobs in other industries. Many U.S. unions have lobbied, along with other interested groups, for both state and federal tax incentives in the United States to make domestic production more attractive. Federal legislation has been introduced to keep production in this country, and several states, including California, have addressed the issue. In an industry where there always have been—and probably always will be—more workers than jobs, runaway production will continue to be an area of concern.

9

SUMMING IT ALL UP

"RETIREMENT" IS A word rarely used by actors. Few actors really "retire." They may not work any longer, but they seldom consider themselves retired.

Consider Gloria Stuart, the eighty-seven-year-old actress who was heralded for her role in the blockbuster film *Titanic*. Ms. Stuart was a popular screen actress in the 1930s, making dozens of films and helping to organize the Screen Actors Guild. Her previous film appearance was in 1946. Then she actually, willingly "retired," to devote time to her family, to traveling, and to cooking. She came out of "retirement" when the wonderful role in *Titanic* was offered to her.

Although most actors may talk of retiring, and may even do it for a while, if the right role comes along, all such thoughts are forgotten.

An actor-comedian who had a long career on stage, once pondered at length over the question, "How do you retire from the theater?" He pondered, perhaps, for two reasons: he did not intend to retire, and he didn't know how. Finally he concluded, "As there is no official 'in' to the theater, there is no official 'out.' I think—I'm not sure—but I think, that when you start tossing away the *Sunday Times* drama section unread, when you no longer feel an urge to see this or an overwhelming desire to study that, when you stop talking shop, when you cease to argue the merits of a production or a performance, when, in short, you're dead—you're retired."

Managing Retirement

Two nonprofit organizations that help with retirement are The Actors' Fund and the Motion Picture Relief Fund, both of which provide care for deserving actors who are in need. Each maintains a dignified, attractive guest home.

The Actors' Fund also maintains a social services department through its offices in New York, Chicago, and Los Angeles. Counseling in areas such as financial, medical, housing, alcohol and drug abuse, part-time employment, money management, and mental health is available. In addition, the problems facing pensioners and prepensioners in the entertainment industry have been addressed. Representatives from the Social Security Administration and State Unemployment offices, Pension and Welfare Fund administrators from the entertainment unions, and actuarial consultants meet with performers to discuss what benefits pensioners are entitled to and how and where to obtain them.

For years, there was no provision for financial benefits upon retirement, and numerous and tragic stories of elderly and indigent actors forced to accept charity after a life of dedication to their profession have been widely publicized.

AFTRA was the first union to win a health and retirement plan for its members. SAG followed, and in 1960 Equity, but only after a Broadway theater blackout. All these plans are financed by employer contributions. Each health and pension fund is jointly administered by representatives of management and labor. Many members have retired with pensions, and thousands benefit from the medical provisions of the plans. Eligibility for pension and the amount received depends in all cases on the amount of covered work the performer has done and the amount of money earned under each union's contracts. Those who have worked in films, television, and on the stage may be eligible to receive a pension from more than one plan.

Retirement for dancers can come a lot earlier than it does for other performers. Most dancers reach the end of their dancing careers in their thirties.

In response to this, Career Transition for Dancers (CTFD), a nonprofit organization, was established in 1985 to help dancers choose, prepare for, and enter new fields. CTFD helps by providing vocational testing and assessment, individual counseling and psychotherapy, financial planning, internships, survival job guidance, assistance in obtaining permanent employment, support groups, career development workshops, special interest seminars and workshops, and financial grants for education, retraining, and new business. Participants in the program have launched successful second careers in fields as diverse as real estate, interior design, psychology, advertising, publishing, arts management, and forestry.

Today, the entertainment profession has developed a number of benefit programs to help its members survive the uncertainty—and, often, brevity—of their careers.

A Final Word

We have attempted to summarize some of the realities of the acting profession—that part of the actor's life not publicized in magazines, the tabloids, or motion pictures. It is not an easy life, and those who choose it must—for their own survival—understand that. If, after experiencing the heartaches, pitfalls, and repeated rejections you still burn with the urge to act, then nothing will keep you from it.

But whether your involvement with acting leads to full-time dedication to the craft or to a pleasurable and rewarding avocation, you will find it fascinating.

The word *amateur* comes from the Latin word "to love." It is possible to find satisfaction in acting "for love," while doing something else to pay the bills.

Pulitzer prize–winning playwright David Mamet has said, "You can pursue fame, but that doesn't mean that you will achieve fame, or that if you get it you'll find it is what you thought it was."

Appendix A

Related Reading

The periodicals and books listed here will offer you a wealth of information about all aspects of the acting profession.

Periodicals

Back Stage (weekly)
770 Broadway
New York, NY 10003
backstage.com

Back Stage West
5055 Wilshire Blvd.
Los Angeles, CA 90036
backstage.com

Hollywood Reporter (daily)
5055 Wilshire Blvd.
Los Angeles, CA 90036
and
770 Broadway
New York, NY 10003
hollywoodreporter.com

Ross Reports (monthly)
770 Broadway
New York, NY 10003
backstage.com

Variety (weekly)
5700 Wilshire Blvd.
Hollywood, CA 90036 '
variety.com

Books

Bone, Jan. *Opportunities in Film Careers.* New York: McGraw-Hill, 2004.

Henry, Mari Lyn, and Lynne Rogers. *How to Be a Working Actor.* New York: Back Stage Books, 2000.

Merlin, Joanna. *Auditioning: An Actor-Friendly Guide.* New York: Vintage, 2001.

Shurtleff, Michael. *Audition.* New York: Walker and Company, 1978.

Appendix B

Organizations

THE FOLLOWING ORGANIZATIONS can help you explore various aspects of the acting profession that interest you.

State and Regional Organizations

Placement Service, Annual Conference
University/Resident Theatre Association (U/RTA)
1560 Broadway, Ste. 712
New York, NY 10036
urta.com

Regional Organizations

New England Theatre Conference (NETC)
PMB 502
198 Tremont St.
Boston, MA 02116-4750
http://netconline.org

Rocky Mountain Theatre Association (RMTA)
State offices in Colorado, Idaho, Montana, Utah, and Wyoming.
rmta.net

Southeastern Theatre Conference (SETC)
P.O. Box 9868
Greensboro, NC 27429
setc.org

Service Organizations

The organizations listed below provide formal or informal assistance in job finding.

Alliance of Resident Theatres/New York
575 Eighth Ave.
New York, NY 10018

Educational Theatre Association
2343 Auburn Ave.
Cincinnati, OH 45219
edta.org

The National Arts JobBank
236 Montezuma Ave.
Santa Fe, NM 87501
westaf.org

Theatre Communications Group
520 Eighth Ave., 24th Fl.
New York, NY 10018
tcg.org

Appendix C

Additional Sources of Information

We have included here the names and addresses of theme parks, which are reasonably stable institutions. Since other theaters might come and go or change management, we have listed sources from which you may acquire up-to-date lists in these areas.

Theme Parks

Astroworld
9001 Kirby Dr.
Houston, TX 77054
sixflags.com/parks/astroworld/index.asp

Bushkill Park
2100 Bushkill Park Dr.
Bushkill, PA 18040
bushkillpark.com

The Dark Continent/Busch Gardens
Entertainment Dept.
P.O. Box 9158
Tampa, FL 33674
buschgardens.com

Hersheypark
Hershey, PA 17033
hersheyjobs.com

The Old Country/Busch Gardens
Entertainment Dept.
One Busch Gardens Blvd.
Williamsburg, VA 23187-8785
buschgardens.com

Six Flags over Georgia
275 Riverside Pkwy.
Austell, GA 30168
sixflags.com/parks/overgeorgia/index.asp

Six Flags Magic Mountain
26101 Magic Mountain Pkwy.
Valencia, CA 91355
sixflags.com/parks/magicmountain/index.asp

Six Flags St. Louis
I-44 & Six Flags Rd.
Eureka, MO 63025
sixflags.com/parks/stlouis/index.asp

Six Flags over Texas
2201 Road to Six Flags
Arlington, TX 76010
sixflags.com/parks/overtexas/index.asp

Walt Disney World/Disneyland
Talent Booking Office
Walt Disney World Entertainment Division
P.O. Box 40
Lake Buena Vista, FL 32830
http://corporate.disney.go.com/careers/index.html

Regional Theaters

Theatre Profiles, published biennially by Theatre Communications Group (see Appendix B), lists performance schedules, artistic statements, names of artistic and managing directors, and other pertinent information for nearly 170 American theaters.

Outdoor Pageants

All outdoor pageants are members of the Institute of Outdoor Drama. Write to the Institute of Outdoor Drama for a list of outdoor dramas. (They are also included in *Back Stage*; see Appendix A.) Institute members hold interviews and auditions at the spring convention of the Southeast Theatre Conference.

Institute of Outdoor Drama
1700 Airport Rd., CB #3240
UNC-Chapel Hill
Chapel Hill, NC 27599-3240
unc.edu/depts/outdoor

Off-Off-Broadway Theaters

A list can be obtained from the Alliance of Resident Theatres/New York (see Appendix B).

Dinner Theaters

Lists are occasionally published in *Back Stage*. For directories of summer theaters, regional theaters, and theater-training programs, contact:

Educational Theatre Association
2343 Auburn Ave.
Cincinnati, OH 45219
edta.org

Equity Theater for Young Audiences (TYA) Companies

THIS LIST IS adapted from the Actors' Equity Association. (Key: PLOTYA— League Member; I—Independent; R—Resident Theater; and T—Touring. * denotes companies that are not currently on a TYA contract.)

Eastern United States

Alabama Shakespeare Festival (R-PLOTYA)
#1 Festival Dr.
Montgomery, AL 36117
asf.net

Alhambra Dinner Theatre (R)
12000 Beach Blvd.
Jacksonville, FL 32216
alhambradinnertheatre.com

Alliance Theatre Company (R-PLOTYA)
Children's Theatre
Robert West Woodruff Arts Center
1280 Peachtree St. NE
Atlanta, GA 30309
alliancetheatre.org

Artpark
450 S. Fourth St.
Lewiston, NY 14092
artpark.net

Arts Power National Touring Company (PLOTYA)
39 S. Fullerton Ave.
Montclair, NJ 07042-3354
artspower.org

Blue Heron Theatre (T)
123 E. Twenty-Fourth St.
New York, NY 10010
blueheron-nyc.org

Fanfare Theatre Ensemble (T-PLOTYA)
102 E. Fourth St., Apt. 2
New York, NY 10003

Fleetwood Stage Company (R-PLOTYA)
44 Wildcliff Dr.
New Rochelle, NY 10805
fleetwoodstage.org

Freedom Theatre (R)
1346 N. Broad St.
Philadelphia, PA 19121
freedomtheatre.org

Gingerbread Players & Jack (T-PLOTYA)
P.O. Box 750296
Forest Hills, NY 11375
gingerbread.org

Growing Stage Company
P.O. Box 36
Netcong, NJ 07857
growingstage.com

The Hippodrome
25 SE Second Pl.
Gainesville, FL 32601-6596
http://thehipp.org

Kennedy Center for the Performing Arts (R/T)
JFK Center Theatre for Young People
2700 F St. NW
Washington, DC 20566
kennedy-center.org/programs/family

Lincoln Center Institute (R/T-PLOTYA)
70 Lincoln Center Plaza, 7th Fl.
New York, NY 10023
lcinstitute.org

Maximillion Productions (T-PLOTYA)
15 Court Sq., #240
Boston, MA 02108

Nashville Shakespeare Festival (R)
1604 Eighth Ave. South, Ste. 250
Nashville, TN 37203
nashvilleshakes.org

New York State Theatre Institute (R/T-PLOTYA)
37 First St.
Troy, NY 12180
nysti.org

North Shore Music Theatre (R-PLOTYA)
Box 62
Beverly, MA 01915
nsmt.org

Pittsburgh Civic Light Opera (R)
719 Liberty Ave.
Pittsburgh, PA 15222
pittsburghclo.org

Pushcart Players (T-PLOTYA)
197 Bloomfield Ave.
Verona, NJ 07044
pushcartplayers.org

*Slim Goodbody Corporation (T-PLOTYA)
P.O. Box 242
Lincolnville, ME 04850
slimgoodbody.com

Stage One (T)
501 W. Main St.
Louisville, KY 40202
stageone.org

*Steamer #10 Theatre (R)
500 Western Ave.
Albany, NY 12203-1621
http://timesunion.com/communities/steamer10

Storybook Musical Theatre (R-PLOTYA)
P.O. Box 473
Abington, PA 19001
storybookmusical.org

Syracuse Stage
820 E. Genesee St.
Syracuse, NY 13210
syracusestage.org

Theatreworks USA (R/T-PLOTYA)
151 W. Twenty-Sixth St., 7th Fl.
New York, NY 10001
theatreworksusa.org

Totem Pole Playhouse
P.O. Box 603
9555 Golf Course Rd.
Fayetteville, PA 17222
totempoleplayhouse.org

Underground Railway Theater
41 Foster St.
Arlington, MA 02174
undergroundrailwaytheater.org

Westchester Broadway Theatre (R)
One Broadway Plaza
Elmsford, NY 10523
broadwaytheatre.com

Midwest United States

Classics on Stage (R)
P.O. Box 25365
Chicago, IL 60625
classicsonstage.com

Drury Lane Oakbrook (R)
Children's Theatre
100 Drury La.
Oakbrook Terrace, IL 60181
drurylaneoakbrook.com/info/assets/children.html

First Stage Milwaukee (R-PLOTYA)
929 N. Water St.
Milwaukee, WI 53202
firststage.org

Imaginary Theatre Company
(Repertory Theatre of St. Louis)
P.O. Box 191730
130 Edgar Rd.
St. Louis, MO 63119
repstl.org/itc/index.shtml

Indiana Repertory Junior Works (R)
140 W. Washington St.
Indianapolis, IN 46204
indianarep.com

M&W Productions Classic Children's Theatre
P.O. Box 511821
Milwaukee, WI 53203
mandwproductions.com

Marriott Lincolnshire (R-PLOTYA)
10 Marriott Dr.
Lincolnshire, IL 60069
marriotttheatre.com

Mixed Blood Theatre
1501 S. Fourth St.
Minneapolis, MN 55454
mixedblood.com

Music Theatre Workshop
7359 N. Greenview Ave.
Chicago, IL 60626
mtwchicago.org

Pyramid Players
930 N. Michigan Rd.
Indianapolis, IN 46268
pyramidplayers.net

Seem to Be Players
940 New Hampshire St.
Lawrence, KS 66044
lawrenceartscenter.com/seemtobe.html

Sesame St. Live (T) (Special Agreement)
VEE Corporation
800 LaSalle Ave., Ste. 1750
Minneapolis, MN 55402
sesamest.live.com

Western United States

ACT: A Contemporary Theatre (PLOTYA)
Kreielsheimer Pl.
700 Union St.
Seattle, WA 98101
acttheatre.org

Casa Mañana Playhouse
3101 W. Lancaster
Fort Worth, TX 76107
casamanana.org

*Denver Center Theatre Company (PLOTYA)
The Denver Center for the Performing Arts
1245 Champa St.
Denver, CO 80204
denvercenter.org

Seattle Children's Theatre (R-PLOTYA)
201 Thomas St.
Seattle, WA 98109
sct.org

Seattle Repertory (R)
155 Mercer St.
P.O. Box 900923
Seattle, WA 98109
seattlerep.org

South Coast Repertory
655 Town Center Dr.
P.O. Box 2197
Costa Mesa, CA 926268
scr.org

Theatre West
3333 Cahuenga Blvd. West
Los Angeles, CA 90068
theatrewest.org

ABOUT THE AUTHOR

DICK MOORE BEGAN his career at the age of eleven months, playing John Barrymore as an infant in the film *Beloved Rogue*. Then known as Dickie Moore, he appeared in more than one hundred films, including such screen classics as *Oliver Twist*, *Sergeant York*, *The Life of Louis Pasteur*, and *Heaven Can Wait*. Many of the films, as well as the *Our Gang* comedies in which he starred, are seen regularly on television and are entertaining new generations of movie buffs.

As an adult, he added radio, television, summer stock, Broadway, and off-Broadway to his credits, as both an actor and director. In addition, he coproduced, wrote, and starred in a short subject called *The Boy and the Eagle*, which was nominated for an Academy Award in 1949. He also produced and directed USO-sponsored overseas tours, served on the acting faculty of the American Academy of Dramatic Arts, and wrote a teleplay produced on NBC. He has also lectured extensively on the theater.

The former child star is currently president of a New York–based communications firm that bears his name and lists among its clients several organizations prominent in the performing arts.

Before forming his own company in 1967, Mr. Moore was creative director for films, meetings, and shows for a leading advertising agency. He also served as public relations director for Actors' Equity Association and editor of *Equity Magazine*.

Mr. Moore, who is listed in *Who's Who in the American Theatre*, *Who's Who in the East*, and *Who's Who in Hollywood*, has served on the State Department Drama Advisory Panel for International Cultural Exchange, the National Council on the Arts and Government, the Drama Panel of the Advisory Commission for the School of Performing Arts, and the Theatrical Advisory Committee to the New York State Attorney General.

Mr. Moore attended Los Angeles State College where he majored in journalism. He served as a sergeant in the United States Army in World War II and was staff correspondent for *Stars and Stripes* in the Pacific Theater.

His book *Twinkle Twinkle, Little Star: And Don't Have Sex or Take the Car*, the story of the old Hollywood studio system as seen through the eyes of its former child stars, was published by Harper & Row in September 1984.

Mr. Moore and his wife, actress Jane Powell, live in Connecticut with their two dogs.